OVERVIEW

Overview

In every business or organization, difficult decisions have to be made in order to adjust to changing economic or marketplace conditions. Companies may have to go through serious organizational changes such as mergers, acquisitions, industrial strife, or downsizing. Whatever direction your organization decides to take, it's important that you communicate effectively with your employees to ensure they understand and support this decision.

During times of significant change, leaders within an organization will have different responsibilities. They may need to convey what the company's new strategic vision is and how they'll achieve it. Leaders should share information in a timely manner and explain how employees' day-to-day activities will be affected. And when planning their communication, leaders need to consider different factors, such as their goals, audience, and strategy.

In this course, you'll examine how different levels of leadership in an organization – senior management, middle management, and frontline supervisors – have distinctive responsibilities for communicating during difficult times. You'll also discover how to create an effective communication plan by using a five-step process that identifies the exact nature of the decisions and the actions needed to implement them.

Then you'll learn how to communicate difficult strategic decisions in face-to-face situations. You'll find out about the importance of explaining your decision and the alternatives explored, informing employees about who was involved in the decision-making process, and ensuring that employees understand the effects of the decision. Finally, you'll be given the opportunity to apply specific communication guidelines in a realistic scenario.

By following the guidelines outlined in this course, you'll have a greater understanding of how to communicate difficult decisions. You'll also learn how to gain the trust and support of your employees, which is crucial in helping your organization overcome any challenges it may be facing.

It's a fact that companies sometimes face challenging times. Economic downturns, mergers, or even extreme growth can present challenges to the way business is conducted. Whatever the nature of these challenges, companies need to respond appropriately in a way that will strengthen them as well as secure their survival.

Sometimes the first response to difficult conditions is to lay off employees. But that should be a last resort. Layoffs can have negative impacts, including a loss of trust among employees, which can be hard to reverse. Before resorting to layoffs, companies should consider other strategies, such a sequence of incrementally more severe cost-cutting actions. These can be highly effective, especially if you gain employee support for them.

If all other options have been exhausted and layoffs are necessary, your company's approach to carrying out the layoffs can still make a difference. With the right approach, you can at least minimize the damage. But challenging times should not be seen as entirely negative. They can also be regarded as an opportunity for the organization to become more efficient and effective.

In this course, you'll learn about how to manage your company's resources effectively in challenging times. It covers strategies for responding to challenging conditions, such as how to get employees to support cost-cutting measures. It offers alternatives to layoffs, and outlines what to do if layoffs are necessary. Finally, it explains how you can strengthen your company by taking advantage of the opportunities difficult times can present.

During times of organizational change, keeping employees engaged and enthusiastic is one of the biggest challenges a manager can face. Whether it's downsizing or rapid growth, large-scale change often generates upheaval and anxiety among the workforce. It's exactly when the organization is going through challenging times that an engaged and productive workforce is especially needed to make change succeed.

Although some loss of motivation is to be expected during times of change, there are strategies you can use to effectively support employees who are struggling to adapt. This course outlines ways to recognize the most common signs of employee stress. It also helps you to understand how your employees are feeling by explaining the common causes of employee frustration and anxiety during transition periods.

By learning about strategies for motivating employees in changing organizations, you'll be equipped to effectively support employees and boost morale. Communicating your support in an honest and supportive way is one of the most important skills you can possess as a manager when your company is experiencing challenging times.

Challenging times may give rise to anxiety, stress, and loss of enthusiasm in managers and those they manage. In this course, you'll learn strategies for reducing stress, techniques for motivating employees, and guidelines for supporting employees during difficult times. These can help you become a more inspired – and inspiring – manager when you most need to be.

CHAPTER 1 - COMMUNICATING DURING DIFFICULT TIMES

CHAPTER 1 - Communicating during Difficult Times
   SECTION 1 - Leadership Communication in Difficult Times
   SECTION 2 - Creating a Communication Plan
   SECTION 3 - Communicating Difficult Strategic Decisions

SECTION 1 - LEADERSHIP COMMUNICATION IN DIFFICULT TIMES

SECTION 1 - Leadership Communication in Difficult Times

During difficult times, decisions need to be communicated effectively to keep relationships between management and employees positive.

Senior management should communicate the conditions driving these decisions, a vision for the future of the company, and information on how changes will benefit employees. It's the responsibility of middle managers to spread the leadership's message in a timely fashion. They should explain the rationale behind the decision and convey employee reactions upward to senior management. Finally, frontline supervisors need to pass on vital information about employees' day-to-day activities.

COMMUNICATING CHANGE EFFECTIVELY

Communicating change effectively

Organizations often go through periods of significant change and turbulence. Organizations may merge with others or be acquired by rival companies. Factories may face the prospect of closure or downsizing due to industrial strife or economic downturns. Alternatively, organizations may branch into new lines of business or have to contend with stringent new regulations. But whatever change is taking place within an organization, it's vital that you communicate decisions effectively to avoid disruption or employee dissatisfaction.

Consider the following situation. Suppose you work as a manager for a printing company that's experiencing a lag in revenue caused by a decline in sales. One of your colleagues speaks informally to some staff members about a possible reduction in work hours.

Soon, rumors start to spread among employees that management is planning to downsize and make significant cutbacks to staff members' salaries and benefits. You notice that team members are fearful about their future with the company, and that their productivity has dropped.

You organize a team meeting to discuss senior management's new strategy of marginally reducing the work week, which will increase efficiency while improving the company's overall competitiveness. However, your team members react defensively. Some complain about being treated unfairly and threaten to walk out if their hours or salaries are cut.

Question

Based on the previous example, what do you think are the benefits of effective communication during times of difficulty?

Options:

1. It enables you to counteract disruptive rumors

2. It can help you get your team members' support and make change implementation easier

3. It may improve your relationship with your team

4. It allows you to reinforce the idea of business-as-usual in your organization

5. It can make your organization more attractive and may improve retention

6. It enables you to make employees feel good about a negative change

Answer

Option 1: This option is correct. Communicating changes in a timely fashion can help stop rumors from spreading and becoming increasingly inaccurate.

Option 2: This option is correct. Effective communication helps employees understand what's required of them, and may decrease their resistance to change.

Option 3: This option is correct. Being open and honest about proposed changes may increase staff members' trust and belief in management.

Option 4: This option is incorrect. Communication during difficult times should highlight how the company's culture or strategy may differ in the future and what positive changes will come about as a result.

Option 5: This option is correct. Keeping employees informed and involved in the process of change can help them stay motivated and committed to the organization.

Option 6: This option is incorrect. You need to make clear the positive aspects and benefits of a proposed change. Employees are unlikely to support any change that's contrary to their own interests or well-being.

LEVELS OF COMMUNICATION

Levels of communication

When communicating during difficult times, leaders need to demonstrate confidence and control, and display a sense of purpose. They must understand and validate employees' reactions. They should focus on building trust with their employees to help them see the positive outcomes of change. And they need to open the lines of communication so that employees can freely discuss the effects of proposed changes.

You may have noted that managers should explain the rationale behind their decision, or that they need to communicate how the decision will affect their employees' day-to-day activities. Leaders also need to support employees by facilitating discussion of planned decisions and by highlighting concerns with senior management.

It's important to recognize that different levels of leadership in the organization have distinctive responsibilities when it comes to communicating during times of change. There are three levels of leadership:

senior management, middle management, and frontline supervisors.

The first level of leadership is senior management. At this level, managers are responsible for reacting proactively to changing market trends. One of their main tasks is to describe the situation driving their decisions. They have to explain the company's new direction and how it will get there. And they have to explain the benefits for employees if the changes are successful.

Describe the situation

Senior managers need to explain the conditions behind any new changes in strategy or direction. Employees will be more receptive if they can understand the forces driving the decisions.

For example, removing incentives without a proper explanation may seem like the malicious actions of an uncaring leadership. By giving a larger overview, however, senior management can place these decisions in the wider context of marketplace forces.

Explain the company's new direction

Once employees have a greater understanding of the marketplace conditions, senior managers then have to explain how the organization will react. This is where senior leaders must communicate their vision for the future of the company, as well as their case for action.

For instance, if a company plans to enter a new market segment, senior management could first explain that the intended market will provide the company with an excellent growth opportunity. Management could then provide details on its analysis of key targets, as well as its market strategy.

Explain benefits for employees

Having communicated its vision for the company, senior management then needs to point out the benefits for the employees if the changes are successful.

For example, if staff members need to take on more work due to downsizing, senior management could explain that the employees will gain more experience, which could help their prospects for promotion.

Take Elizabeth, for example. She's an operational manager at a pharmaceutical company that's planning to merge with one of its main rivals. At a meeting with other senior and middle managers, she outlines the reasons for the merger, citing spiraling research and development costs.

She then explains how the merger will help them become one of the most competitive pharmaceutical companies in the industry through a more streamlined production process. Elizabeth also discusses the introduction of new performance-related benefits for employees once the merger has successfully been completed.

The second level of leadership is middle management. At this level, managers are expected to pass on information and communicate the leadership message to other staff members or departments. One of their main responsibilities is to communicate decisions to employees in a timely fashion. They also need to explain to their reports the rationale behind the leaders' decisions. And finally, they should relay employee reactions upward to senior management.

Communicate decisions in timely fashion

After finding out from senior management what the decision is, middle managers need to pass on vital information quickly in order to ease the fears of the company's employees. Leaders at this level should be alert for any rumors about proposed changes and correct them as necessary.

Middle managers must also share as much information as they can to demonstrate that they're being open and honest.

Explain rationale behind decisions

When detailing senior management's plans, middle managers must convey the reasons for these decisions. Many departments or staff members may be unaware of marketplace forces or problems with their company's infrastructure or strategy. If middle managers explain these issues, other departments are more likely to understand and support changes within the company.

For instance, if an organization plans to close a branch or plant, middle managers could explain that senior management's aim is to cut costs.

Relay employee reactions upward

Employees may have fears, questions, or objections about planned changes to a company's strategy. It's important for middle managers to communicate these objections to senior staff so that they can be addressed directly. This can also help to gauge how easy it will be to implement the planned changes.

For example, if a company plans to introduce a new pension plan, middle managers could speak with employees to determine their level of understanding or acceptance of these changes. They could then share this information with senior managers to find out how to communicate the benefits of the decision.

Miguel works as a middle manager at the pharmaceutical company from the previous example. After consulting with some of the senior staff regarding the planned merger, he quickly organizes a staff meeting with some of the supervisors and employees.

At the meeting, he presents aspects of the merger, explaining the need for increased efficiency and a broader portfolio of products to increase the company's market share.

Miguel also invites questions from the participants. Some of the supervisors raise concerns about how resources will be shared and if layoffs will be required as part of the merger. Miguel then brings these concerns to the attention of senior management.

Frontline supervisors make up the final level of leadership. Supervisors have direct contact with employees, and are responsible for explaining how company change affects employees' day-to-day work practices.

During difficult times, employees will depend on the leaders they interact with most to find out about the impact of new decisions. That's why frontline supervisors need to be well informed about these decisions.

And as supervisors will often have developed good relationships with their employees, they can sometimes apply a more personal touch when delivering difficult news such as layoffs.

Consider Andrew. He's in charge of one of the production line teams at the pharmaceutical company. During a staff briefing, Andrew explains that as part of the merger, some staff members may be required to relocate to their new partner's plant site.

He also points out that some production staff will need to complete training before they start manufacturing some of their clients' products.

Question

Match the examples of typical communication actions to the corresponding management level. Each level may have more than one match.

Options:

A. Lou explains R&D costs have risen, forcing the closure of an assembly plant

B. Ben tells workers there will be promotion opportunities after a merger to increase market share

C. Sam explains to employees a plan to file for bankruptcy, saying the firm must reorganize to be profitable again

D. Jan tells employees shifts will be cut by two hours a day

E. Liz relays employees' concerns about her firm's merger to senior managers

Targets:

1. Senior management
2. Middle management
3. Frontline supervisors

Answer

Lou and Ben use communication actions appropriate for senior management. Lou describes the conditions driving the decision. Ben outlines one of the benefits for employees of the proposed change, and explains where the company is going.

Sam and Liz use communication actions appropriate for middle management. Sam explains the rationale behind the decision. Liz shares information and conveys employee reactions upward to senior management.

Jan uses a communication strategy appropriate for frontline supervisors by clarifying important day-to-day information.

SECTION 2 - CREATING A COMMUNICATION PLAN

SECTION 2 - Creating a Communication Plan

An effective communication plan is critical in providing a framework for explaining and implementing your organization's decisions. When creating your plan, you first need to analyze your company's background and the root causes of its current situation.

You should then identify a specific goal related to your organization's vision. With this goal in mind, you then need to analyze your audience to find out how different segments will be affected by the decision. This will help to develop messages that are relevant to each segment.

Next, you have to create strategies that will outline your general direction and develop measurable objectives in line with these strategies. Finally, you need to consider tactical aspects, such as appropriate tasks and media, and the overall cost of putting your communication plan into effect.

DEVELOPING A COMMUNICATION PLAN

Developing a communication plan

Communicating bad news to employees is one of the most difficult and important challenges organizations will face. Employees will understandably be concerned and want exact details on what and why these changes are taking place. They may also ask "When will this decision be implemented?" or "How will I be affected?" To answer these questions effectively, it's critical to create a communication plan that will clearly outline your organization's decision.

You can use five main steps to create an effective communication plan. First, review your company's background and current situation. Second, identify your company's goal. Third, analyze your audience. The fourth step is to create a set of communication strategies and objectives that will help you achieve the goal. Finally, decide on what tactics you can use to get your message across.

Creating a communication plan can help to clarify your organization's purpose. And by outlining your decision in writing, it will give your organization's strategic vision a greater sense of reality, which may encourage employees' acceptance of change.

Question

Place the key steps for creating a communication plan in order.

Options:

A. Review the background and situation
B. Identify the company's goal
C. Analyze your audience
D. Create strategies and objectives
E. Decide on tactics

Answer

Review the background and situation is ranked the first step. First, you have to find out about your organization's current situation and the reasons behind this.

Identify the company's goal is ranked the second step. Second, you need to specify what the intended result of your company's decision is.

Analyze your audience is ranked the third step. Third, you must analyze and segment your audience to make sure you address specific concerns.

Create strategies and objectives is ranked the fourth step. Fourth, you outline what direction your organization should take and the steps that can help it reach its goal.

Decide on tactics is ranked the fifth step. Finally, you need to focus on the tactical aspects of your plan, such as costs and the appropriate media to use.

BACKGROUND, GOAL, AND AUDIENCE

Background, goal, and audience

The first step when creating your communication plan is to conduct a background and situation analysis. Your review could ask questions about your organization such as "What's our current position?," "How did we get here?," and "What message do we want to send to our clients?" Also, be sure to clarify the communication needs and identify key issues that your plan must address.

Ask questions

When carrying out a background review, you need to examine the company's current circumstances by asking questions. Is your company downsizing or streamlining its production process? Is it entering a new market? Or is it being acquired by or merging with a new partner?

Clarify communication needs

Understanding your organization's current circumstances can also help you to clarify your communication needs.

For example, suppose your organization has had to send its production lines offshore to cut costs. Your communication plan will need to explain the forces behind this decision. It should also demonstrate how your organization will support its employees, and how they may benefit from it.

Identify issues

Once you've clarified the background and identified the communication needs, you need to highlight specific issues that your plan must address. This involves analyzing the root cause of your company's current situation. This analysis also helps narrow the scope of your plan.

For instance, if your organization is entering a new market, you could find out if there are any regulations you should be aware of, and if so, how to comply.

Take Rachel, for example, a manager at a computing company that's acquiring one of its rivals. She's designing a communication plan and starts by analyzing the background of her company's planned acquisition. She finds that her company is trying to take advantage of a larger global presence to increase sales.

She then recognizes that her communication plan needs to make clear who employees in both companies will be working for, and how they'll fit in. And she notes that the plan will have to deal with negative aspects of the acquisition, such as the layoff of some members of staff.

Rachel also analyzes her company's situation, taking into account a gradual downturn in sales in the five previous quarterly returns. She's aware that her plan will need to address this issue by outlining how her company will combat this steady decline.

The second step in creating your communication plan is to identify your company's goal. Once you've established the background and circumstances of the change, you need to outline the aims or results your organization wishes to achieve.

Goals may be stated in general terms, but should be focused enough to indicate what the desired end result should be. For example, a wholesale company's goal could be to become the largest distributor of computer accessories in a particular area.

Bear in mind that the goal you set out for your organization is not itself the act of communicating; rather, it's what the communication plan will help you accomplish.

Consider Denise, a manager at an online gourmet food company who is responsible for profitability in her area. Having analyzed her business's recent increase in orders, she comes to the conclusion that the company should expand into other markets.

In her communication plan, she outlines a goal of introducing a new line of organic snack bars into her company's range of products.

The third step in creating your communication plan is to analyze your audience. It's vital to identify your audience to help focus your message. With your goal in mind, you need to segment your employees into distinct categories. And once you've done that, you should then assess your audience to determine what's relevant to each segment.

Identify your audience

When creating your communication plan, consider who'll be affected by your organization's new plan or strategy. Try to take into account all employees within your organization.

Think about the people whose knowledge, attitudes, or behavior must be changed in order to reach your goal.

Segment employees

Having considered all the employees within your organization, you then need to segment them into distinct groups. Classifying employees according to different groups allows you to create more targeted messages.

For example, employees in your organization could be profiled according to their level of seniority. They might be permanent or contract workers, or be based in the company's headquarters or at an overseas location.

And keep your goal in mind when segmenting your employees. For example, if your goal is to enter a new market sector, you might target your message to salespeople or marketing managers within your company.

Assess your audience

Once you've profiled your target employees, consider what makes new information credible for them. Who or what could motivate change or action? And what is the most appropriate method of communicating your goal?

For instance, sending a newsletter to all employees about changes to managerial positions may be inappropriate for factory floor workers who are unlikely to be affected by these changes.

Consider Omar, an information officer at a telecommunications company. He's responsible for outlining how the company will begin offering a cell phone service in addition to its existing Internet and landline services. He first creates a list of all the people involved with his organization, such as employees, contractors, and other stakeholders.

He then segments his company's employees into different categories and lists five main employee groups: HR managers, marketing managers, engineers, customer care supervisors, and call center agents.

Having broken employees into separate groups, Omar then takes into account how these groups will be affected by the introduction of this new service. For example, some employees will require training in mobile telephones. With this in mind, he plans new training videos to keep customer care staff up to date with the new service.

Question

Match each action to the step in creating a communication plan where it belongs. Each step may have more than one match.

Options:

A. Jen notes poor call-handling skills as a main cause of customer dissatisfaction

B. Nick knows that those affected by a plant closure need to hear how the company can help them

C. Chen focuses on how his company can return to profitability by year-end

D. Noel identifies employees who'll be affected when his firm relocates one of its units

E. Olga plans to use a presentation to inform production line staff of changes to the QA process

Targets:

1. Review background and situation
2. Identify goal
3. Analyze audience

Answer

Jen and Nick both review their company's background and situation. Jen looks at root causes of her company's current situation, and Nick considers his communication needs based on the company's circumstances.

Chen identifies a goal by outlining the main results his company wants to achieve.

Noel and Olga both analyze the audience for their communication plans. Noel identifies which employees will be impacted by the company's decision. Olga assesses her audience by considering which medium is appropriate for her communication plan.

STRATEGIES AND TACTICS

Strategies and tactics

The fourth step when developing your plan is to create strategies and objectives to help your company meet its communications goal. An effective strategy is a well-defined plan of action that outlines the direction your organization needs to take. An objective, on the other hand, is a measurable step or goal taken to achieve your communications strategy. When planning your objective, you'll also need to establish key messages tailored to both general and specific audiences.

Your strategies and objectives should consist of realistic actions that will enable your company to reach its goal. For example, suppose an organization intends to introduce a new employee benefits package. One possible strategy might be to show employees the advantages of the new package.

When creating your objectives, concentrate on the quantifiable steps that can help you execute your strategy. For example, if your strategy is to ensure employees accept a new benefits package, an objective could be to determine their current level of understanding of planned changes.

During the objectives phase, you should think about what key messages you want to send to your audience. A clear message can focus and support your communication plan. For instance, a general message when introducing a new benefits plan might be "To implement a plan which will decrease costs and increase coverage options." A more specific message may show what different employee segments would gain from the proposed benefits package.

For example, take Dana, an HR manager at an insurance company. She has to draft a communication plan describing a decision to restructure one of the firm's regional divisions. To achieve this goal, she outlines a strategy to minimize employee departures related to fears over the restructuring.

To reduce staff losses, she decides her objective will be to pinpoint main areas of concern about the restructuring process.

Finally, Dana creates a message to support her main objective – "There will be no redundancies or demotions as a result of this restructuring process."

The final step in creating a communication plan is to decide on what tactics you can use to achieve your objectives. These tactics are specific activities and methods that will help implement a strategic decision. You'll need to consider what tasks need to be carried out. You'll also have to determine what media you'll use. And you should keep in mind the cost of implementing your plan.

Tasks

Your tasks will vary depending on your objectives. For example, if your objective is to identify employees' concerns about a merger, you could use a survey to find out their level of understanding of the decision. You could also organize town hall meetings to address their concerns directly.

Media

There are several different types of media that can help get your message across to different employee segments. For instance, you could use newsletters, brochures, intranet sites, or worksheets.

When deciding on your media, consider whether you want to get feedback about the decision. Also think about which media will have the greatest impact and which can convey complex messages most effectively.

Cost

Budgeting is a tactical element that you'll need to keep in mind when creating your communication plan.

For example, you may need additional staff, such as consultants, to help devise your message. You may also need to document the cost of developing communication materials such as newsletters, mailings, or web sites.

Consider Brian, an operations manager for a travel agency which is closing some of its branches due to a downturn in bookings. One of his main objectives is to ensure all employees are kept up to date with details of the closure.

In his communication plan, he schedules a series of meetings between managers and supervisors to discuss when and how the closures will take place. He also plans to send mailings with specific details of severance packages to employees' homes.

Question

Match each action to the appropriate step in developing a communication plan. Each step may have more than one match.

Options:

A. Ann decides that part of her company's goal to enter a new market will be to ensure it complies with regulations within that market

B. Lars aims to have sales staff trained on a product management program within a month to help develop a new marketing campaign

C. Rob creates a newsletter to keep employees informed about the progress of the company's cost reduction plan

D. Iris plans a town hall meeting to provide opportunities for questions and answers during her company's downsizing

Targets:

1. Create strategies and objectives
2. Decide on tactics

Answer

Ann and Lars develop strategies and objectives to support their goals. Ann identifies one method of helping her company reach its goal. Lars outlines a specific and measurable objective.

Rob and Iris both use tactics to help them achieve their goals. Rob has decided on a specific communication vehicle, while Iris plans specific tasks.

Question

Match each action to the corresponding step in creating a communication plan.

Options:

A. Lori finds out what has caused her company's sales to drop

B. Troy specifies that his company should reduce transportation costs by 20%

C. Jean considers how a planned merger will affect managers and supervisors differently

D. Ian creates a message outlining how managers will be minimally impacted by a restructuring process

E. Raj calculates how much an intranet site explaining his company's acquisition will cost

Targets:

1. Review background and situation
2. Identify the company's goal
3. Analyze your audience
4. Create strategies and objectives
5. Decide on tactics

Answer

Lori identifies the main issues her plan must address, which is part of reviewing the background and situation.

Troy defines the main goal his company should achieve.

Jean analyzes her audience by segmenting employees into different groups.

Ian establishes a segment-specific message to help support his objective.

Raj considers his budget, which is a tactical element of his communication plan.

SECTION 3 - COMMUNICATING DIFFICULT STRATEGIC DECISIONS

SECTION 3 - Communicating Difficult Strategic Decisions

When communicating a difficult decision to employees, there are a number of important guidelines you should keep in mind. Be clear about what decision has been made and the rationale behind it. Describe what alternatives were explored, and why the final decision is the best solution for your organization and its employees.

Discuss who was involved in the decision-making process, and how the decision will affect employees' daily routines. And finally, make sure that employees fully understand the changes resulting from your company's decision.

Remember that throughout this communication process, you must avoid using business jargon or technical details. Showing empathy for your employees and listening to their concerns during the communication process are also vital.

COMMUNICATING DECISIONS TO EMPLOYEES

Communicating decisions to employees

Communicating difficult decisions can have a negative effect on your employees. They may react with shock, anger, or objections to the company's decision. However, using an effective communication approach can help you gain your employees' trust and continued commitment to your company's goals. It may also get employees to focus on the tasks that need to be performed, regardless of the distractions caused by these decisions.

You should keep a number of key guidelines in mind when communicating difficult strategic decisions. You need to state clearly what the decision is and explain it, as well as the process for arriving at that decision. You should describe what alternatives were explored and note who was involved in making the decision. Explain what impact the decision will have, and make sure employees understand the strategic change.

There are also some general guidelines you should follow to ensure your message is clear and to show support for your employees.

First, avoid jargon and technical details. Using buzz words such as "turnkey solutions" will do little to help employees understand the day-to-day realities of the organization's new direction. To get your message across more succinctly, outline in plain terms the specific actions, objectives, or behaviors expected as part of your new strategy.

Second, listen to your employees and show empathy. Don't assume your employees are as confident as you are about the outcome of the decision. Give them an opportunity to express any fears about the organization's decision. But be careful not to dismiss employees who voice their concerns as change resistant. Instead, show understanding of their feelings while emphasizing the need for change.

Question

How can you communicate difficult decisions effectively?

Options:

1. Explain the decision and the rationale behind it

2. Discuss other ideas that were considered during the decision-making process

3. Point out that employees need to accept the decision or the company's goal will fail

4. Clarify which members of staff were involved in the decision-making process

5. Provide details about how the decision will affect employees' day-to-day activities

6. Explain that you are also concerned about the rationale behind the decision

7. Ensure that staff members are fully aware of the proposed change or decision

Answer

Option 1: This option is correct. Discussing decisions and the background behind them, such as marketplace trends, can help employees see the bigger picture.

Option 2: This option is correct. By discussing other ideas, you can demonstrate that the decision was given due consideration.

Option 3: This option is incorrect. While you should explain the need for change, employees shouldn't feel pressured into accepting a decision. Instead, focus on the long-term benefits for both the employee and the organization.

Option 4: This option is correct. It's important to explain who is responsible for developing your organization's new strategy.

Option 5: This option is correct. To implement strategic changes more effectively, employees need to know what their new responsibilities or duties are.

Option 6: This option is incorrect. You should try to be positive about the decision and encourage employees to see the long-term benefits.

Option 7: This option is correct. Employees need to have all the details so they can understand the full implications of the decision.

DESCRIBING THE DECISION

Describing the decision
The first guideline for communicating a difficult decision is to explain what the decision actually is and the rationale behind it. Employees are likely to have a negative reaction to unexplained changes. That's why it's better to give an explanation that people may dislike than no explanation at all.

When describing the decision, be honest, and provide as much information as you can about changes to the organization's direction. Remember to use your judgment if discussing confidential information or sensitive issues, such as changes to health care plans or benefits packages. Employees are also more likely to accept a difficult decision if they understand the reasons behind it. For example, you could explain background issues, such as changing marketplace forces, rising production costs, or new regulations.

Take Martha, for example. She's a manager at a publishing company and is meeting with one of her employees, Lucas, to outline a recent decision to streamline the company.

Martha begins by outlining the reason for the decision. She states that in the last year alone orders have fallen by over 10%, mainly due to poor global economic conditions. She also highlights the publisher's inefficient distribution service, which has caused several delays in its delivery schedule.

Martha goes on to explain that to reduce costs, senior managers have decided to consolidate distribution services into one centralized location. She details when the publishers' main operations will move to the company's main warehouse. And she points out that as part of this process, employees will have the option of taking a reduction in hours or relocating to the central warehouse.

Question

Conrad is a supervisor at a medical supply company, and has to explain a decision to his employees regarding changes to a quality assurance process.

Which statement best implements guidelines for communicating a difficult strategic decision?

Options:

1. "New health and safety legislation has recently been introduced to ensure our equipment is regularly inspected and monitored."

2. "Because of new health and safety legislation, production line staff will require training on designated equipment and will have to keep detailed maintenance logs."

3. "From next year, production line staff will not be allowed to operate designated equipment without completing an accredited training course."

Answer

Option 1: This option is incorrect. This statement highlights a reason for the decision but fails to explain what has been decided.

Option 2: This is the correct option. This statement outlines the decision as well as the rationale behind it.

Option 3: This option is incorrect. This statement does announce the decision but neglects to provide the reason behind the new training requirement.

ALTERNATIVES AND PEOPLE INVOLVED

Alternatives and people involved

The second guideline when communicating difficult strategic decisions is to describe what alternatives were explored. You need to show that your organization's critical decision has not been made lightly. Employees should know what other options were considered and why your company's decision is the best choice for its current circumstances.

Demonstrating that your organization has taken the time and effort to explore other alternatives can convey your concern and respect for your employees. When describing alternatives that were rejected, point out why the chosen decision will be better for the organization and its employees.

For example, if your company has decided to reduce employees' hours, you could explain that decision-makers had also considered unpaid vacation days. You could then highlight how this decision avoids scheduling problems and may improve employees' work-life balance.

The third guideline is to note who was involved in your organization's decision. Telling employees who was included in the decision-making process shows that your company is accountable for its decisions. It also shows that you're willing to provide as much information as you can.

Consider Martha's meeting with Lucas. Having explained the decision and its rationale, she then talks about what alternatives her organization considered, as well as the people involved. Follow along as she explains this to Lucas.

Martha: The decision to centralize our operations has not been an easy one for us. We consulted extensively with strategic planners and regional managers, as well as our HR managers, to find the best solution.

Martha is empathetic.

Lucas: But this seems like a drastic measure. Isn't there some other way we could cut down costs?

Lucas is angry.

Martha: Well, we did carry out a feasibility study to find out if job sharing would work in our current circumstances. And we also looked into offering unpaid vacations.

Martha is apologetic.

Martha: However, both of these alternatives would have been quite difficult to implement. Job sharing would have required additional training for some members of staff. Unpaid vacation, on the other hand, would have caused major disruption when coordinating different team members' tasks.

Martha is sympathetic.

Martha: That's why we believe that a reduction in work hours is a good option. It will cause only minor disruption and it will allow you to keep getting a regular salary.

Martha is confident.

In the previous example, Martha did well by outlining what alternatives the company looked into. She explained why it rejected these alternatives and pointed out the benefits of its final decision. Martha also provided additional information by discussing who was involved in the decision-making process. And throughout her discussion, Martha empathized with her employee and didn't dismiss his concerns.

Question

Penny is outlining her company's decision to redeploy some of its employees to another department.

Which statement best implements guidelines for communicating a difficult strategic decision?

Options:

1. "We looked into reducing hours, but our operations and planning managers thought redeployment would be better because it keeps employee salaries at their current levels."

2. "Some of the managers decided that by redeploying employees, we could improve their knowledge of our internal processes."

3. "Our operations and planning managers had a strategic vision of improving interdepartmental communication."

Answer

Option 1: This is the correct option. This statement outlines what specific alternative was considered and how the final decision may benefit the organization and its employees. It also shows who was involved in the decision.

Option 2: This option is incorrect. This option only vaguely refers to who was responsible for the decision, and it doesn't mention what alternative was explored.

Option 3: This option is incorrect. This statement uses business jargon and doesn't specify what alternatives the managers considered.

EXPLAINING EFFECTS AND CHANGE

Explaining effects and change

The next guideline to follow when communicating a difficult decision is to be sure to explain what impact the decision will have on your employees. It's crucial that you provide details about what their day-to-day reality will be once the decision has been implemented.

By outlining specific changes to employees' duties or responsibilities, you're more likely to improve their receptiveness to the decision. When communicating bad news such as layoffs, be honest. Although you may feel uncomfortable talking about sensitive issues, don't make the mistake of withholding important information.

And make sure to express how your organization will support employees. You need to demonstrate that your organization is geared toward their well-being, despite the negative aspects of the decision.

The final guideline is to make sure employees fully understand the change that your organization is proposing. You need to encourage questions from employees to find out what their main areas of concern are. This will also help to clarify any inaccurate information they may have heard from their colleagues or the media.

Consider Martha and Lucas's meeting again. Follow along as Lucas discusses the decision to centralize the company's operations.

Lucas: I'm worried about my workload after this merger. I mean, I'm busy enough as it is.

Lucas is concerned.

Martha: Well, we understand this is a huge issue for all of our employees. Let me just assure you that we'll try to make this transition as smooth as possible.

Martha is sympathetic.

Martha: If you did decide to relocate to our main facility, you would need to take on some different responsibilities to fit into the work flow process that's currently in place.

Martha is sympathetic.

Lucas: And how am I supposed to cope with these different responsibilities?

Lucas is anxious.

Martha: Well, we would have to train you in the product management software used in the central warehouse. And we're sure the skills and experience you would bring would be key in improving our distribution services. Do you have any other questions about this decision?

Martha is confident.

In the previous example, Martha made sure to inform Lucas how the decision would affect him by pointing out that training would be required.

She focused on the outcome the company was seeking as a result of the decision, and tried to make sure that Lucas understood all the implications of the decision.

And Martha showed empathy for Lucas, while making sure to avoid technical language that may detract from her message.

Question

Antonio is a manager at a telecommunications company. He's meeting with one of his employees who's concerned about a decision to restructure the Sales Department.

Which statement follows guidelines for communicating a difficult strategic decision?

Options:

1. "Going forward, you'll be responsible for managing a cross-functional team and for leveraging resources in order to increase the uptake of our integrated services."

2. "There's nothing to worry about. You'll just need to make sure that our sales staff are up to speed with our new integrated service."

3. "After the Sales Department is restructured, you'll be responsible for managing a large group of salespeople who will be cross-selling our television, phone, and Internet services."

Answer

Option 1: This option is incorrect. This statement uses a lot of jargon and doesn't make clear how the change will affect the employee.

Option 2: This option is incorrect. This statement doesn't demonstrate an understanding of the employee's concerns.

Option 3: This is the correct option. This statement outlines in clear terms how the decision will affect the employee.

Question

Gina is an HR manager at a hotel and has to explain a decision to introduce a three-day working week to the hotel's housekeeping staff.

Which statements follow guidelines for communicating a difficult strategic decision?

Options:

1. "Competition from other hotels in the area has had a major impact on bookings, and unfortunately we need to cut staff hours in order to reduce our costs."

2. "We've decided to be proactive and tackle this situation head-on. A reduction in the working week is mission critical and should result in a win-win situation."

3. "The general and housekeeping managers also considered voluntary layoffs, but we know this would have caused employees a lot of stress."

4. "Your schedule will be coordinated with those of your colleagues, so we expect you to be as flexible as possible to ensure there's always someone available."

5. "While your weekly hours will be cut, this won't affect your benefits package. Do you have any questions about this?"

Answer

Option 1: This option is correct. This statement outlines in plain terms the decision to cut staff hours, as well as the rationale behind this decision.

Option 2: This option is incorrect. Using business jargon isn't appropriate when trying to explain decisions that affect frontline staff.

Option 3: This option is correct. Explaining who was involved in the decision, as well as alternatives explored, is important, as it shows the decision was given due consideration. This statement also demonstrates empathy for the hotel employees.

Option 4: This option is incorrect. While this statement outlines one effect of the decision, it shows a lack of concern for the employee.

Option 5: This option is correct. Outlining how a decision will impact employees and making sure they understand any resulting changes are vital when communicating tough decisions.

CHAPTER 2 - MANAGING RESOURCES DURING DIFFICULT TIMES

CHAPTER 2 - Managing Resources during Difficult Times
SECTION 1 - Strategies for Responding to Difficult Times
SECTION 2 - Alternatives to Layoffs
SECTION 3 - Laying Off Employees
SECTION 4 - Opportunities for Organizations in Difficult Times

SECTION 1 - STRATEGIES FOR RESPONDING TO DIFFICULT TIMES

SECTION 1 - Strategies for Responding to Difficult Times

Three strategies for responding to difficult times are cutting unnecessary costs, building relationships with customers and suppliers, and valuing good employees.

Winning employee buy-in to cost-cutting solutions is imperative because solutions are more effective when employees support them. To win that support, you need to communicate the importance of cost reduction to employees, involve employees in generating ideas, and act on the best ideas.

RESPONDING TO DIFFICULT TIMES

Responding to difficult times

Whether due to an economic downturn or a period of extreme growth, companies sometimes face difficult financial circumstances that require them to reduce their spending. Knowing how to respond can help companies avoid drastic measures such as layoffs, which should be a last resort. In fact, several strategies can be used as a first line of defense during difficult times to reduce expenditures. Companies can cut unnecessary costs, build relationships with customers and suppliers, and value good workers.

The first strategy is to cut unnecessary costs. While this may seem obvious, companies often overlook potential savings by not reviewing current spending. As a manager, you can begin by looking to reduce travel expenses, reduce office space, eliminate unprofitable advertising, and save on small items.

While some travel is necessary, some isn't. Once you start looking, you may find various ways to reduce travel expenses:

- ask people to come to you,
- use technology, such as video and teleconferencing, e-mail, or project web sites to facilitate collaboration among remote contributors, and
- seek competitive pricing for travel.

Ask people to come to you

You can reduce expenses by asking people to come to you. For instance, a manufacturer may organize a trade show. Bringing clients to one location to showcase products and provide information saves on the cost of traveling to each client.

Use technology to facilitate collaboration

When possible, use technology to facilitate collaboration. An international bank, for instance, may elect to use videoconferencing to have board meetings with executives from each of its worldwide locations.

Seek competitive pricing for travel

You may also be able to reduce expenses by seeking competitive pricing for travel. For example, senior managers attending annual meetings at each of their company's national locations can carefully investigate options and get the most competitive travel rate before making arrangements.

Changing locations or reducing your current office space can help save money. Can your company reduce office space? Money spent to support your physical work location doesn't result in your company making more money. Investigate ways to save money on rental and leasing fees, equipment, and workstations.

Allowing employees to telecommute is another possibility. This may be considered a perk to employees and will reduce the office space, and associated costs, you need to provide.

For example, a training organization offers distance training to clients. This allows it to save on the travel expenses that would be required to send instructors to the clients. And because instructors are also working remotely, the company saves on costs associated with providing office space for them.

Another way to cut unnecessary costs is to eliminate unprofitable advertising. Review your advertising efforts and determine which ones are providing value. If the exposure isn't generating value, cut the advertising.

Concentrate instead on advertising that does provide value. Consider carefully whether you're making the best of free advertising opportunities using social media.

For example, an investment firm decides to reach out to tech-savvy customers of all ages using various appropriate social media channels.

Finally, you can reduce spending by looking for ways to save on small items. Saving money on the little things such as printer cartridges, paper, and postage can add up to big savings.

For instance, a company learns that a recycling program offered by its supplier can reduce the price of replacing and disposing of used printer cartridges.

A second strategy to use during difficult times is to build relationships with customers and suppliers. If your company is experiencing difficult times, your customers and suppliers are probably experiencing them too. This presents a potential mutual dependency that can be beneficial. For instance, once relationships are established, you may be able to ask for temporary price cuts, order fewer materials more frequently to relieve pressure on suppliers, and find out which customers to keep when times get tough.

Ask for a temporary price cuts

When your organization has well-established relationships, it may be possible to ask for and receive a temporary price cut during tough economic times.

For example, suppliers may agree to a price cut instead of losing a customer.

Order fewer materials more frequently

Every organization needs to buy materials or supplies from other companies. If your demands are straining the capacity of suppliers during difficult times, your organization can relieve pressure by ordering fewer materials more frequently. This will help to build a positive relationship with this supplier.

For example, suppose a supplier explains that purchasing the inputs to fill your company's order is creating financial hardship and it's having trouble filling orders. If your company agrees to accept fewer supplies more frequently, the supplier will be able to remain viable. Agreeing to such an arrangement could lead to a reciprocal favor when your organization needs help.

Know which customers to keep

It's imperative your organization knows which customers to keep. Keeping your most important customers is in your organization's best interest.

Suppose, for instance, your customer base is large but many customers don't contribute to profits. Knowing this, you can focus your efforts on working to build and maintain positive relationships with your best customers.

A third strategy to get you through difficult times is to value good workers. Your high performers are your best resource, and in hard times it's especially important that you don't lose them. To pursue a strategy of valuing good workers, you'll first need to keep specific performance records. Then you'll need to identify your top performers. And finally, you'll want to reward these top performers appropriately.

Keep specific performance records

Be sure to keep specific performance records to collect information about what skills and traits your company values in its employees. For instance, you may want to track who can operate what equipment, or who can perform multiple roles. Or perhaps good communicators with excellent interpersonal skills are most important. Specifics such as who's a good team player or days absent can also be useful information if layoffs become necessary.

Identify top performers

Identify top performers so, if decisions need to be made about who to keep and who to let go, you'll be able to make informed decisions. Identify top performers by comparing what your company values in employees with what individual employees are contributing.

Reward top performers

Speak with top performers to find out how you can reward them for their efforts. For instance, some employees may like to work flexible hours, while others may want to work from home.

It's important to note that all of these strategies can and ideally should be used during good times too. Cutting unnecessary costs is always beneficial. Building relationships during good times is likely to be easier and can be a support system to be relied on during difficult times. Value good workers all the time and, during difficult times, they'll be more likely to be loyal.

Question

Which actions are appropriate to take during difficult times?

Options:

1. Administrative staff members are instructed to negotiate better prices with office suppliers

2. A company always knows who its most profitable customers are

3. A purchasing manager negotiates a lower price for materials in exchange for ordering fewer items at once

4. Detailed performance reviews allow an organization to identify its best employees and offer them work at home privileges

5. A pay freeze is used to minimize the impact of a forecast economic downturn

6. As a preliminary measure, managers are asked to select two employees to lay off

Answer

Option 1: This option is correct. Reducing the price of small items is one appropriate way of cutting unnecessary costs.

Option 2: This option is correct. Part of building relationships is knowing which customers need to be maintained during difficult times.

Option 3: This option is correct. Being able to negotiate for better prices and ordering fewer materials more frequently are actions that are possible when your company has built good relationships with suppliers.

Managing During Difficult Times

Option 4: This option is correct. When good workers are valued, they're more likely to be loyal during difficult times.

Option 5: This option is incorrect. Measures such as pay freezes should be a final response during difficult times, not a pre-emptive one.

Option 6: This option is incorrect. Organizations should look for ways to reduce unnecessary costs before resorting to layoffs.

WINNING EMPLOYEE BUY-IN TO SOLUTIONS

Winning employee buy-in to solutions

During challenging economic times, many cost-cutting solutions can be implemented before resorting to such drastic measures as pay cuts and layoffs. But, for cost-cutting solutions to be most successful, you need the support of your employees.

Three steps can help you build employee support: communicate the importance of cost reduction, involve employees, and act on the best ideas.

First, you need to communicate frequently and openly with employees about the importance of cost reduction. Let them know that sacrifices are necessary to help the organization remain financially viable.

Providing regular updates will build confidence and trust that management is acting in the employees' best interests.

Where changes are necessary, it's important to explain why and to be specific about how the change will impact employees. For instance, provide details about which segments of the workforce will be affected and whether the change is permanent or temporary.

Next, devise a clear communication plan for informing employees about cost-cutting measures. Communication plans will vary depending on such factors as the type, size, and location of the organization. But these three guidelines for developing an effective communications plan always apply: determine who will communicate the information, establish when the communication will happen, and define how the information will be communicated.

Who will communicate information

First, determine who will communicate information. Designate official sources of information, such as a spokesperson or a Communications Department, to share information with employees. This helps employees know what to believe and cuts down on rumors and erroneous information and their negative effects.

When communication will happen

Establish when communication will happen and be consistent. If it's time for a regular communication and there's no news to report, tell employees that. Otherwise an interruption to regular communication may be misunderstood and have an unintended negative impact.

How information will be communicated

Define how official information will be communicated. A variety of communication channels exist, but not all channels are appropriate for all types of messages. Take some time to define which channel to use for which type of information. For instance, if voluntary early retirement is being offered, one-on-one communication is more appropriate than a company-wide communication.

Finally, provide facts as needed to keep employees informed. Employees want to know the details, no matter what the change. So, as you communicate change, share facts in an honest, respectful, and open way.

Consider the example of a financial consulting firm that has started looking at ways to reduce costs in preparation for an anticipated economic downturn. Knowing that employee support is essential, it has appointed a communications specialist to keep employees informed of changes.

During a meeting with employees, the organization learns of an inefficient procedure that, if improved, will reduce time wasted doing repetitive tasks.

Since then, employees have been receiving frequent updates from the communications specialist about changes to the procedure and the anticipated effects on how they'll do their jobs.

Question

Which examples follow guidelines for communicating the importance of cost reduction?

Options:

1. Employees receive monthly updates about what's going on in the organization

2. A designated communications officer conveys official information to employees

3. Affected employees are advised of the specific changes to the overtime policy

4. Because there is nothing new to communicate, the company spokesperson skips his weekly update

5. Individual employees are asked at a general meeting to indicate whether they're interested in early retirement

Answer

Option 1: This option is correct. Communicating frequently with employees will help them be more accepting of changes when these are necessary.

Option 2: This option is correct. Establishing official sources of information is a good way to counteract the rumor mill and make sure employees get accurate information.

Option 3: This option is correct. It's important to provide details so employees aren't left to speculate about how they'll be affected by cost-reduction measures.

Option 4: This option is incorrect. Be consistent with updates. Otherwise harmful rumors and speculation can grow.

Option 5: This option is incorrect. Sensitive issues need to be handled discreetly not in public meetings.

A second method for building employee support is to involve employees in developing cost-cutting measures by working with them to regularly identify cost-saving opportunities. Your company can elect to do this in a variety of ways – departmental meetings, brainstorming sessions, focus-group meetings, regular staff meetings, or even using a suggestion hotline. Employees' involvement is important because they'll be more likely to be supportive of solutions they helped develop.

As you look for ways to reduce costs, exercise caution because there are serious issues at stake, including job security. If, for example, cost-cutting measures become more drastic and include voluntary retirement or job losses, there can be potential legal implications.

Finally, consider using a facilitator to generate ideas and opportunities for savings. This can be more effective because employees may be hesitant to share openly with managers and supervisors.

Recall the financial consulting firm working to reduce wasted time by improving a procedure? Team leaders are asked to invite employees to provide their input about how to improve the procedure. Team leaders also continue to solicit input. When potential layoffs are mentioned, the team leader leading the discussion assures the employees that they aren't an option. Instead she encourages the team to focus on other possible ways to save money.

Another team leader appoints a facilitator to lead these discussions with her team. She knows that her team is suspicious of management and probably won't share openly with her or members of the communications team.

Question

Which statements describe appropriate ways to involve employees in developing cost-cutting opportunities?

Options:

1. A department is brainstorming to find ways to make its procedures more efficient

2. Managers are careful to focus on ideas that don't require layoffs or pay cuts

3. A facilitator is brought in to lead the discussion on cost-saving opportunities

4. Managers meet to draw up a list of potential cost-saving opportunities for employees to review

5. A department head has a team meeting to talk about opportunities to cut costs by introducing job sharing

Answer

Option 1: This option is correct. Involve employees in the discussion of how to reduce costs by soliciting their input, perhaps through meetings, brainstorming sessions, or individual contributions.

Option 2: This option is correct. It's not appropriate to involve employees in discussions that focus on layoffs and pay cuts. These measures are drastic and need to be handled carefully.

Option 3: This option is correct. Sometimes employees are hesitant to contribute freely in the presence of mangers. In these cases, facilitators may be able to gather better information.

Option 4: This option is incorrect. It's best to involve employees from the beginning. Otherwise, you may miss out on ideas and information only employees have insight on.

Option 5: This option is incorrect. Job sharing is quite drastic and isn't an option that should be discussed as a possibility with employees.

A third method for gaining employee support for cost-cutting solutions is to act on the best ideas that have been generated – that is, those that offer the best combination of payoff and effort. Typically, the best ideas to act on are opportunities that focus on saving energy, that will overcome operational inefficiencies, or that allow you to share best practices.

Remember the consulting team looking to improve a procedure? With the help of employees, several options for improving the procedure are generated. Management reviews the options and chooses the idea that offers the best improvement with the least amount of effort.

Question

Which statement demonstrates good practice for acting on the best ideas?

Options:
1. Managers meet to review ideas and select the cost-saving opportunities that will cost the least to implement and provide the greatest benefit
2. Managers meet to submit one idea from each department for implementation
3. Executives ask senior managers to focus on downsizing as the only way to save costs

Answer

Option 1: This is the correct option. The best cost-saving opportunities are those that offer a high payoff with low effort.

Option 2: This option is incorrect. Only the best ideas, those that provide a high payoff at low effort, should be chosen for implementation.

Option 3: This option is incorrect. During difficult times, organizations should first look for opportunities to save on energy costs, improve efficiency, and share best practices.

SECTION 2 - ALTERNATIVES TO LAYOFFS

SECTION 2 - Alternatives to Layoffs

Layoffs are costly in many ways and can have a serious negative impact on employees left behind. So your company should do whatever it can to avoid them. Thankfully, alternatives are available such as reducing staff-related costs.

Staff-related savings can be made through measures related to compensation, benefits, and work restructuring.

BENEFITS OF AVOIDING LAYOFFS

Benefits of avoiding layoffs

As you manage resources during difficult times, it's hard to rule out options – even layoffs. However, there are good business reasons to avoid layoffs, if possible.

Suppose a massive layoff is planned by an electrical utility, as a response to difficult times. Although it has invested heavily in recruiting and training new employees, the utility follows the last hired, first fired rule and lays most of the new employees off. Affected employees are paid severance to lessen the blow.

Unfortunately, this has a negative impact on productivity. Following the layoffs, the company begins to experience unacceptable delays in getting work done. Customer service is deteriorating. It turns out the smaller workforce can't handle the workload. Remaining workers are suspicious and wonder when they'll be laid off, and the drop in morale also slows productivity.

In addition to the cost of implementing the layoffs, the utility also faces increased labor costs when it needs to hire some of these employees back to meet service demands.

Many workers agree to return only if they receive higher salaries.

Question

Given the example of the utility company, what do you think some of the benefits of avoiding layoffs might be?

Options:

1. You avoid losing the investment you've made in hiring and training employees
2. You avoid the negative impact layoffs have on the organization
3. You avoid additional costs associated with implementing layoffs
4. You avoid having to do additional performance reviews
5. You avoid losing customers who are offended by your organization's approach

Answer

Option 1: This option is correct. It will likely cost you more in the future to replace the lost workers when growth resumes.

Option 2: This option is correct. You preserve morale, gain trust, respect, and long-term loyalty by being seen as avoiding layoffs.

Option 3: This option is correct. Costs associated with layoffs include severance payments, increased unemployment insurance rates, and time spent to consider and implement layoffs.

Option 4: This option is incorrect. Your organization should be conducting regular performancereviews. And to be prepared in case layoffs are required it should be tracking specific traits and abilities that it values most in employees.

Option 5: This option is incorrect. If you're legitimately laying off employees as a last resort, there's no reason to expect that your customers will be offended and take their business elsewhere.

REDUCING STAFF-RELATED COSTS

Reducing staff-related costs

Given that layoffs are damaging and should be an absolute last resort, what can your organization do to avoid layoffs? Staff-related cost reductions are one method to help you avoid layoffs. These fall into two categories – reducing staff-related expenses and restructuring work.

Reducing staff-related expenses is one alternative to layoffs. Reductions can be made to compensation, benefits, or both. Although better than layoffs, your employees aren't likely to be happy about staff-related cost reductions. But you can help employees accept these changes by explaining that they are necessary to avoid more drastic measures. Then work to implement the changes with as little disruption to employees as possible.

Begin by considering how to reduce compensation expenses. Four progressively severe measures are commonly used: withholding raises, suspending bonuses, implementing mandatory unpaid leave, and instituting a salary cut.

Withholding raises

One thing your company can do is withhold raises. Consider starting with new hires and then apply the policy to all employees.

For example, a company that usually gives raises at the end of its probationary period could announce that it will withhold these raises until it's stronger financially.

Suspending bonuses

Your company may choose to suspend performance bonuses. Temporarily eliminating bonuses can be an effective way to save money. Just be careful, however, because this can have a demotivating effect on employees.

For example, a software development company is experiencing an extended lull in custom work – its main profit-generating activity. Programmers are told that until the company sees signs of improvement, it won't be able to pay performance bonuses.

Implementing mandatory unpaid leave

Implementing mandatory unpaid leave can be an effective way to save money without decreasing hourly wages.

For example, a construction company experiencing an unanticipated lull in work decides that each employee will stay home one day a week until work picks up.

Instituting a salary cut

Instituting a salary cut is a fairly drastic way to save money during difficult times. This is typically done as a percentage of current wages or salary.

A company may choose to implement this across the entire organization, for instance, by reducing pay by 10%.

Question

Sequence the examples of measures that can be taken to reduce compensation expenses before resorting to layoffs from least to most drastic.
Options:
A. Recent hires are advised that they won't be getting the automatic pay raise that typically accompanies the end of probation
B. A development organization suspends performance bonuses, but vows they'll be reinstated as soon as possible
C. Workers at a manufacturing plant are sent home for two weeks' unpaid leave during a slow period
D. A company reduces all salaries by 5%
Answer
Recent hires are advised that they won't be getting the automatic pay raise that typically accompanies the end of probation is ranked the first measure. Withholding pay raises is the first measure organizations should consider to reduce compensation expenses. Ideally, start with the newest employees and then expand the policy to all employees.

A development organization suspends performance bonuses, but vows they'll be reinstated as soon as possible is ranked the second measure. Suspending bonuses won't be popular, but this is the next measure to consider after withholding pay raises.

Workers at a manufacturing plant are sent home for two weeks' unpaid leave during a slow period is ranked the third measure. Mandatory unpaid leave is another way to reduce compensation expenditures during difficult times. This measure is more drastic than suspending bonuses.

A company reduces all salaries by 5% is ranked the fourth measure. Making across-the-board pay cuts is the most drastic way of reducing staff expenditure short of layoffs. It should only be used when less severe measures to reduce staff-related expenses have been exhausted.

The second category of staff-related expenses is benefits. Various measures can be taken in this area to save the company money:

- review the existing benefits plan and make sure your company is getting the best value for its money,
- phase out less important benefits based on employee input, and
- reduce employer contribution to benefits, bearing in mind that a reduction of 5% or 10% would likely be acceptable to employees and yield big savings for your company.

Review existing benefits

One way to save money on benefits is to review existing benefits. For example, suppose a human resources team reviews its company's existing benefits plan and discovers that some of what it's paying for is rarely being used. It speaks to its benefits provider and negotiates a better combination of benefits that will offer a better value to employees and be less expensive for the company. Additionally, human resources compares what other benefits providers can offer.

Phase out less important benefits

Another way to save money is to phase out less important benefits. A company, for instance, may ask departmental managers to meet with employees to find out which benefits they value the most. It turns out that, if given a choice, employees would rather phase out life insurance and long-term disability and keep vision and dental coverage.

Reduce employer contribution to benefits

Companies can also save money by reducing employer contributions to benefits. A company looking for ways to save money on benefits implements a roll back of its contribution to benefits coverage by 5%. While employees aren't happy about the change, it's far more acceptable than losing benefits.

Normally, laws exist regarding what benefits a company must provide. So, whatever your company plans to do, it has to proceed carefully. For example, there may be laws governing minimum health care coverage. Check the laws in your jurisdiction to make sure all your proposed changes are legal before making them.

Question

Identify examples of actions that can help reduce expenditures on benefits.

Options:

1. An organization's human resources specialist meets with various benefits providers to secure a plan that combines essential coverage at the most competitive rate

2. Following a review of benefit usage and consultation with employees, a company decides to eliminate coverage of private hospital rooms

3. A company decides to decrease its contribution to vision coverage by 5% and all other benefits by 10%

4. Following a review of benefit costs, an organization decides to eliminate the most expensive benefits 5. Without consulting with employees first, an organization reduces vision and dental coverage

Answer

Option 1: This option is correct. Your organization should compare what various benefits providers can offer to make sure it gets the best coverage at the best price.

Option 2: This option is correct. Consult with employees to learn what benefits are most or least important to them. Then tailor your benefits coverage to meet employee key expectations.

Option 3: This option is correct. Reducing the amount your organization pays toward employee benefits is an effective way to reduce the cost of benefits.

Option 4: This option is incorrect. Simply eliminating the most expensive benefits may not be the best solution, especially if those benefits are vital to employees or if their elimination is illegal.

Option 5: This option is incorrect. Employees are likely to be upset by the reduction to benefits. If benefits need to be reduced, it's important to involve employees in the decision so they'll be more supportive of the changes.

RESTRUCTURING WORK

Restructuring work

Work restructuring can also be a viable alternative to layoffs. Savings on staff-related costs can be gained by making such changes to the structure of how work is done.

Many actions can be taken to restructure work and reduce labor costs. Some of the more popular measures include reassigning work when implementing a hiring freeze, allowing flexible work arrangements, offering unpaid leave, reducing work hours proportionate with pay cuts, and discontinuing the use of temporary and part-time employees.

Reassigning work

Reassigning work during a hiring freeze can reduce labor costs. For instance, if your company commits to a six-month hiring freeze and employees leave the company, it can redistribute work to existing employees instead of filling the positions. For the time being, this can be an effective way to save on labor costs.

Allowing flexible work arrangements

If you allow flexible work arrangements such as the option to work part-time permanently or temporarily, some employees may be happy to do so. For instance, this might be an amenable situation for parents looking to spend more time with small children or mature employees who want to transition into retirement slowly.

Offering unpaid leave

Offering unpaid leave may also be appealing to some employees. Given the opportunity to take a temporary leave from work, for example, may be a perfect option for individuals who want to take an extended holiday, return to school, pursue a personal goal, or take care of a sick family member.

Reducing work hours proportionate with pay cuts

Reducing work hours proportionate with pay cuts is an option for reducing labor costs. You may have a harder time finding volunteers, but it can be a viable solution when demand for your product or service has decreased. For example, instead of resorting to layoffs for some employees, a reduction in hours for all employees can be a way to save labor costs, retain the employees you've invested in, and avoid the negative impact of layoffs.

Discontinuing the use of temporary and part-time employees

Similar to a hiring freeze, discontinuing the use of temporary and part-time employees can save you money if you don't replace the workers, but instead redistribute their work until difficult times pass. For example, if your company has been using part-time employees to manage administrative tasks for its development teams, it can let go of the part-time employees and reassign the work to the team.

Each work restructuring measure has its drawbacks, but all measures have the same benefit – they reduce labor costs. Used carefully, work restructuring can help your organization avoid layoffs.

Question

One way to reduce labor costs is to give full-time employees the option to temporarily work part time.

What are other examples of work restructuring to reduce labor costs?

Options:

1. When an employee leaves, reassign her duties rather than fill the position

2. Some employees are allowed to take unpaid leave to pursue volunteer opportunities

3. A company reduces all its employees' hours by 20%, thus reducing the wage bill by a fifth

4. Employees with performance problems and who meet the criteria for dismissal are let go

5. Temporary employees are given a dismissal notice, and their work is divided among permanent employees

6. Pay cuts are implemented for employees with fewer than five years with the company

7. Hours are increased to meet demand but wages aren't

Answer

Option 1: This option is correct. Choosing to reassign duties instead of filling the position is an example of an action that might be taken during a hiring freeze.

Option 2: This option is correct. Unpaid leave is a great way to reduce labor costs while also offering employees a chance to pursue personal interests.

Option 3: This option is correct. Reducing wages and hours proportionately across the board is an equitable way to save on labor costs.

Option 4: This option is correct. Be careful that you have the legal right to terminate employees before taking this action to reduce labor costs.

Option 5: This option is correct. Savings can be made by discontinuing the use of temporary or part-time employees and having their work absorbed by permanent employees.

Option 6: This option is incorrect. Pay cuts are quite drastic and should be a last resort. If they are necessary, reduce pay across the board to avoid resentment and feelings of being treated unfairly.

Option 7: This option is incorrect. This would save money, but won't make your employees very happy. You may lose employees or their loyalty and respect.

SECTION 3 - LAYING OFF EMPLOYEES

SECTION 3 - Laying Off Employees

When layoffs have become unavoidable, you need to be able handle them effectively. A three-step process can help you plan and implement layoffs effectively.

First, plan the workforce reduction. This involves documenting your financial conditions, identifying the goal of the layoffs, specifying essential and inessential job functions, and establishing a time line for carrying out the layoffs.

Second, select which employees to let go using these criteria: length of service, job necessity, and job performance. Third, you need to convey the bad news to those being let go. When meeting the individual, have another manager present, be supportive but firm about the decision, be able to explain the basis for the decision, be prepared to cope with employee shock, and offer outplacement assistance.

PLANNING FOR LAYOFFS

Planning for layoffs

While layoffs should always be a last resort, they are sometimes unavoidable. But that doesn't mean the organization should carry out these layoffs in an impetuous and ill-considered way. Layoffs should be conducted in a carefully planned, well-thought out manner. Planning for layoffs should involve department managers, human resources, and ideally, legal counsel. Strict rules guide the process of laying off employees and companies that fail to follow them can find themselves in a legal battle.

If your organization has exhausted its options and layoffs are unavoidable, a three-step procedure can help you lay off employees in an appropriate way. The first step is to plan the workforce reduction, then decide how to select employees, and finally, tell employees affected by the layoff.

The first step, planning your workforce reduction in advance, will increase the effectiveness of the layoffs. This preparation step mostly involves collecting information.

Performing several activities can help you plan an effective workforce reduction:
- document the organization's financial conditions to fully establish why the layoffs are necessary,
- identify the goal of the layoffs in terms of labor costs to be achieved, and state the number of employees the organization is presently overstaffed by,
- identify essential job functions and skills to help make sure you retain employees with the ability and skills to operate effectively,
- identify unnecessary jobs that can be eliminated, and
- establish a time line for carrying out the layoffs, as acting quickly and decisively can minimize the negative effects of layoffs.

Consider this situation. After exhausting all the alternatives, senior managers in a struggling manufacturing company realize that downsizing is necessary. A team is put in place to plan the layoffs and members are meeting to discuss progress. Follow along to find out what the team has accomplished so far.

Jill: Hi everyone! No doubt we've all been working hard getting the data we need to make informed decisions about how to manage the downsizing. Travis, why don't you start?

Travis: Sure, Jill. I've been working with finance to crunch the numbers. Without a serious reduction in labor costs, our company could face receivership in as little as eight months. We need to reduce our workforce by 20% in order to avoid this.

Jill: Thanks for the work you've put into that, Travis. Now, Philippe, I know you've been working closely with Travis to determine how we can best achieve that staff reduction.

Philippe: That's right. I determined which jobs need to be maintained and compiled a list of essential skills to support them. The list can be used in conjunction with performance reviews to determine which employees are most essential to retain. I also identified jobs that could be eliminated or merged.

Jill: So what kinds of skills and abilities do we need to keep?

Philippe: Experienced employees with knowledge of complicated machinery and processes are a valuable asset. Because production will also be slowing down, we can use these employees in several capacities without increasing the demand on their time.

Jill: That's very helpful! This is going to be tough, but knowing that there'll be clear reasons for our decisions is a comfort. So, given all this, what's the time line we're looking at?

Travis: Well, we've determined that we can do this all at once, and it should be completed within the next 30 days.

Question

A cable company is feeling the impact of an economic downturn. Although it has taken measures to reduce expenses, these haven't been enough to solve their problems. A small team has been put together to plan the layoffs. Access the learning aid Cable Company Layoffs and review section 1 to find out what the team did to plan for the layoffs.

Which elements of an effective plan have the team planned for?

Options:
1. Document financial conditions
2. Identify the goal of the layoffs
3. Identify essential job functions and skills
4. Identify unnecessary jobs
5. Establish a time line

Answer

Option 1: This option is correct. In order to make appropriate decisions and justify the layoffs, it's important to document the organization's financial situation at the time the layoffs are done. The company's CFO did this.

Option 2: This option is correct. A goal must be set to provide guidance for the layoffs. The company knows it must reduce its workforce by 25%.

Option 3: This option is correct. Knowing which skills and job functions are critical to the company's success will help you determine who should be kept. In this case, technical skill and field experience are most important.

Option 4: This option is incorrect. The cable company should have also reviewed its current functions to determine if any jobs are or will be unnecessary.

Option 5: This option is incorrect. By not creating a time line, this team can't effectively conduct the layoffs. Ideally, layoffs should done promptly and in quick succession, if more than one round is necessary.

SELECTING EMPLOYEES FOR LAYOFF

Selecting employees for layoff

Having identified the general workforce reduction, you then need to decide how to select which employees to let go. This step involves making objective comparisons based on three criteria. In order of priority, they are length of service, job necessity, and job performance.

Length of service

First, consider length of service. Generally, employees with the least seniority should be laid off first. However, there are exceptions to this. For instance, if you've just hired an experienced person with the credentials your organization needs, you may not want to lay off this employee, despite the short tenure with the company.

Job necessity

Determining job necessity is the next consideration. For example, if your organization has decided to refocus on the activities that provide its competitive advantage, some jobs may become unnecessary.

Job performance

Managing During Difficult Times

Finally, you may use job performance as a way to decide who to lay off. Of course this will only work if your company has up-to-date and detailed information about employees. This will enable your company to factor in performance history in making decisions about who to retain and who to let go.

Recall the manufacturing company experiencing difficult times? Some time has passed since the last meeting when the workforce reduction plan was conceived. Now the team is meeting to decide how they will select which employees to lay off. Follow along as the team meets to decide how to select individuals to lay off.

Jill: We've completed a competitive analysis and found that our success lies in our custom work. Recently we've branched out into mass production. Now, to return to more profitable activities, senior management has decided to downsize to refocus on custom work.

Philippe: What does that mean for employees?

Jill: Well, some of our recent hires are less skilled than our veteran employees. We'll need to retain our experienced workers to perform the custom work.

Travis: That makes sense. But shouldn't we also consider people's performance?

Jill: Yes. After considering seniority, and the current necessity of the job, we'll consider job performance.

Philippe: OK. So an employee with the least seniority, performing an unnecessary job, with, comparatively, the least stellar performance will be laid off first?

Jill: Yes. This way, we'll retain our most experienced, necessary, top performers.

Question

At the cable company, decisions are being made about who to lay off. The team is currently reviewing three employees.

Then, based on what you've learned, rank the candidates in the order in which they should be laid off.

Options:

A. Roberto

B. Tara

C. Lex

Answer

Roberto is ranked the first candidate to be laid off. Because Roberto has the least experience, is performing an unnecessary job, and has the least impressive job performance, he'll be laid off first.

Tara is ranked the second candidate to be laid off. While Tara has more seniority than Roberto, she has less than Lex. Tara's job is necessary, but her performance isn't as good as Lex's. As such, Tara will be the second candidate to be laid off.

Lex is ranked the third candidate to be laid off. Lex has the most experience, job relevance, and the highest performance rating. If necessary, Lex will be laid off last.

ADVISING EMPLOYEES OF LAYOFFS

Advising employees of layoffs

Having planned the reduction and made the selection, the final step is to tell the employees affected by the layoff. This is a difficult task that requires diplomacy, respect, and consistency. Several guidelines should be followed: if possible, have another manager present as you meet with affected employees individually, be supportive but firm in the company's decision, be able to explain the basis for the decision, be prepared to cope with employee shock, and offer outplacement assistance.

Meetings should be held with employees individually and, ideally, two members of management should be present. This will help you deliver the news effectively.

During the discussion, no matter where the discussion goes, remain supportive of employees to help them deal with the information. However, you must also firmly defend the company's decision to lay off employees. Layoff action needs to be decisive to be effective and if you show doubt in the company's decision, it can make the situation even more difficult.

The third guideline is to be able to explain the basis for the decision. If asked, your reply must be well-reasoned and logical – not hasty or poorly thought out.

Make sure you can explain possible recall or rehire rights, severance benefits if they apply, as well as any health insurance conversion rights and other compensation or monetary issues.

You also need to be prepared to handle employee shock, surprise, or inability to take in the information being conveyed.

Finally, offer outplacement assistance if available. Explain what types of assistance are available to help employees transition into new jobs. Perhaps your company will contact or distribute resumes to appropriate potential employers.

The team working on layoffs at the manufacturing company is now in the process of actually laying off employees. Jill and Philippe are meeting with individual employees to tell them that they've been selected to be laid off. Follow along as they speak with Anita, an employee.

Jill: Welcome, Anita. Have a seat. I suppose you're wondering about why we are here.

Jill is serious.

Anita: Well, yes. I think I have a pretty good idea, but I hope I'm wrong.

Anita is serious.

Philippe: As your manager, I wanted to be the one to inform you that due to unfortunate circumstances, and after exhausting all other options, the company has decided it must lay off some employees.

Philippe is supportive.

Managing During Difficult Times

Anita: Oh no, I knew it! What am I going to do? I need this job!

Anita is panicked.

Jill: I know this is hard. At this time, the company can't maintain its current production and manpower levels. If we don't make these reductions, everyone will soon be out of a job.

Jill is concerned.

Philippe: We'll be sending resumes to other employers who might be able to use your skills. We hate to lose good employees, and we're going to provide references and referrals to help you find another job.

Philippe is compassionate.

Anita: And what about my benefits?

Anita is concerned.

Jill: For the next six months, you'll be eligible for basic prescription drug, dental, and vision care coverage. If you get coverage elsewhere sooner, your coverage here will end then.

Jill is supportive.

Question

Which statements are appropriate when telling an employee he's being laid off?

Options:

1. "Your resumes will be distributed to all employers who could make use of your particular skill set."

2. "I know this is a lot of information to take in; we'll take it slow and I'll answer all of your questions."

3. "If we don't focus our efforts on our core strengths, the company may not survive."

4. "I agree, the company's explanation doesn't make sense."

5. "Joyce, it will be just you and me in this meeting today."

Answer

Option 1: This option is correct. If your organization is planning to offer outplacement assistance, tell affected employees this.

Option 2: This option is correct. Employees may very well be shocked. You need to be prepared to help them handle the information.

Option 3: This option is correct. You need to offer a reason for the decision, if asked.

Option 4: This option is incorrect. It's important to support the company's decision, otherwise you can

create doubt and layoffs will be less effective.

Option 5: This option is incorrect. Ideally, you should have at least two members of management in the meeting to tell employees about layoffs.

SECTION 4 - OPPORTUNITIES FOR ORGANIZATIONS IN DIFFICULT TIMES

SECTION 4 - Opportunities for Organizations in Difficult Times

Difficult times can present opportunities to strengthen your organization. Take advantage of difficult times by developing strategic alliances that will benefit your organization, review your business plan to align with market conditions, re-evaluate business practices to eliminate hidden costs, and advance valued employees.

STRENGTHENING ORGANIZATIONS

Strengthening organizations
Remember that while difficult times present threats, they can also present opportunities to strengthen your organization. As a manager whose organization is experiencing difficult times, your goal should be to help your company thrive rather than just survive. Difficult times provide the opportunity for businesses to become more efficient and effective. So why not take advantage of opportunities that exist?

Consider all your options and be strategic when making business decisions. Conducting business in this way will help you identify opportunities that exist for your organization during difficult times. Your organization will then be better prepared to grow and capitalize when the difficult times turn around.

You can respond positively to difficult times by taking a number of specific actions to help your organization identify and take advantage of opportunities. These actions include developing strategic alliances and reviewing your business plan. Also, you should be re-evaluating business practices for hidden costs, and advancing valued employees if you've had to freeze recruitment.

Developing strategic alliances can be a great way for your organization to flourish during difficult times. Alliances, even with competitors, can enable your organization to streamline production or produce complementary products that make each organization's products more attractive to consumers. Specifically, with strategic alliances, you can collaborate to develop or extend products and create mutual referral agreements. Alliances will be most advantageous if you align with your best competitors and base alliances on common goals.

Collaborate to develop or extend products

Your organization can collaborate with other organizations to develop or extend its products or services. Combining your organization's strengths with those of another organization can allow both organizations to benefit.

For instance, companies might work together on a project or certain types of work and deliver a product or service consumers want that neither company could provide on its own.

Create mutual referral agreements

Create mutual referral agreements with individuals or companies. Finding reputable companies to enter into mutual referral relationships with will help both parties get business. It's crucial that you respect and have faith in the companies you recommend or else your own reputation and business could suffer by recommending an inferior supplier of a product or service.

For example, a retailer of pleasure crafts and recreational vehicles has a mutual agreement with a trailer manufacturer. The companies sell complementary products and have agreed to refer each other to customers.

Align with your best competitors

Align with your best competitors to share best practices. It's only logical that if you're going to share information, you'll want to share information with an organization that has something to offer your organization. Learning from the worst competitors in the market won't help your organization gain an advantage.

For example, partnering with the cutting-edge engineering firm in agricultural methods might be a good idea for a food manufacturer. And it might make sense for a music producer to partner with a prominent recording studio.

Base alliances on common goals

It's important to base alliances on common goals. Before entering a strategic alliance, your company needs to take the time to make sure its goals are complementary to those of the company. Otherwise, your organization might end up in a situation where communication and collaboration is difficult if not impossible.

A company that wants to enter a new market, for instance, may want to join forces with a company already in that market. In return, the company entering the market can offer its expertise in technical matters.

Another way you can take advantage of difficult times is to use this time to question your business plan. You may need to adjust your organization's business plan to meet the new realities or even new potential presented by difficult times.

Now is the time to do a competitive advantage analysis to make sure your organization is focusing its efforts on what really makes it profitable.

Also, to take advantage of opportunities, you must know what's truly an opportunity for your organization. If a competitor fails, you may be able to buy equipment for a reduced price. However, if you don't need the equipment, buying it could strain your finances and threaten your organization's financial stability. What first looks like an opportunity might not be.

Your organization can also take advantage of difficult times by re-evaluating business practices to find hidden costs.

Can you improve existing practices to make them more efficient or economical? Look for ways to cut costs that have been previously overlooked. Remember, cutting costs will save your organization money in good times too.

For example, you may find that your organization is paying extra for a premium membership to an industry think-tank journal. However, you have your own analysts who can provide the information you're entitled to in the premium membership. Upon renewal, your organization decides that a basic membership will adequately meet its needs.

Another measure often used to respond to difficult times is to implement a hiring freeze. While this is a negative action, the upside is that it gives you an opportunity to promote qualified individuals from within the organization.

Advancing employees from within will likely make these employees happy and improve loyalty. And your organization saves money on recruiting new employees during difficult times.

For instance, a company facing difficult times needs to fill some vacancies right away, but has implemented a hiring freeze. When the positions are advertised within the company, many deserving and qualified applicants apply. This is a win-win situation for the organization and its employees.

Question

Which actions are examples of taking advantage of difficult times to improve the organization?

Options:

1. Competitors decide to work together temporarily to share the costs of specific research

2. Knowing that its competitive advantage comes from the quality of its products, an organization improves its quality control procedures to enhance quality

3. A review of the company's travel policy highlights several areas where unnecessary costs can be cut

4. Suitable employees are promoted during a recruitment freeze

5. A company buys a competitor's liquidated assets even though it's not sure what it will do with them

6. A company hopes to gain referrals from other companies by recommending companies that provide complementary products

Answer

Option 1: This option is correct. Competitors can work together in a limited capacity to the benefit of both companies during difficult times.

Managing During Difficult Times

Option 2: This option is correct. Knowing where your value comes from will help your organization protect what provides its competitive advantage.

Option 3: This option is correct. Sometimes reviewing regular business practices can reveal opportunities to eliminate hidden costs.

Option 4: This option is correct. A hiring freeze may be used as an opportunity to reward high performers with promotion.

Option 5: This option is incorrect. Buying assets at discounted prices is only an opportunity if your organization can use them to be more competitive. Otherwise it could be a burden for your organization.

Option 6: This option is incorrect. References can be beneficial, but a mutual agreement must be reached or your company may not benefit.

CHAPTER 3 - MANAGING ATTITUDES DURING DIFFICULT TIMES

CHAPTER 3 - Managing Attitudes during Difficult Times
   SECTION 1 - Reducing Stress in Difficult Times
   SECTION 2 - Motivating Employees in Changing Organizations
   SECTION 3 - Supporting Employees through Difficult Times

SECTION 1 - REDUCING STRESS IN DIFFICULT TIMES

SECTION 1 - Reducing Stress in Difficult Times

Occupational stress can be overwhelming when organizational and technological changes are rapid. These changes make employees feel anxious and insecure. As a manager, you need to recognize signs of stress your employees may display during difficult times of change. These include a tendency to voice more complaints, display negative emotions, and be less focused on their work.

But before you can help your employees reduce their stress, you need to use techniques to reduce your own. To relieve your own stress, establish priorities, be realistic about what you can do, eliminate interruptions, and learn to delegate. To reduce employee stress, keep track of workloads, help employees organize their work, and negotiate for more resources when possible.

STRESS: CAUSES AND SYMPTOMS

Stress: causes and symptoms

Modern lifestyles are generally perceived to be more stressful than those of previous generations. Much of the additional stress comes from changes in how work is organized. Levels of occupational stress have tended to rise as the pace of organizational and technological change has increased and work has become more complex.

Stress is often a response to economic downturns and the changes that come with them. These include corporate collapses, streamlining operations, mergers, downsizing, and large-scale layoffs. Increasing job insecurity makes employees more and more fearful and anxious. Also the increasingly competitive nature of local and overseas markets and the globalization of trade and commerce put extra pressure on domestic businesses, which in turn adds to employee stress.

Stress can negatively affect employee well-being, performance, and productivity. It's essential, as a manager, to be able to recognize the signs of stress in your workforce.

A manager who can recognize and alleviate stress is certainly more likely to have a committed and productive workforce.

There are three common signs of employee stress. When employees are suffering from excessive stress, they may have a tendency to voice more complaints, display negative emotions, and lose focus on work. Being aware of these symptoms of stress can help you be more sensitive to the issue, which is the first step toward dealing with it effectively.

Voice more complaints

One of the first signs that employees are experiencing occupational stress is a rise in the number of work-related complaints. There may also be an increase in health-related complaints leading to a rise in absenteeism.

Display negative emotions

During times of transition, employees commonly experience fear of loss. This may be loss of job, title, supervisor, or career opportunities. The most common emotion during times of change is anxiety. The strain of uncertainty may lead to anger, which may manifest itself as general irritability or negative comments about coworkers, management, or customers. Other common emotions during times of change are disbelief and sadness.

Lose focus on work

Employees suffering from excessive stress may take longer than usual to complete their tasks or make mistakes that they normally would not. These may be signs that the pressure of change or of a given situation is taking its toll and that you, as manager, need to act.

Consider this example. Jenny is a manager at a small food manufacturing company. Recently, the company was acquired by a larger food manufacturer and some employees were let go as part of merging the operations of the two companies.

In the last few weeks, Jenny has noticed that there have been more quality control issues on the production line than usual. She's also gotten a number of complaints from employees about the levels of morale and cooperation on the factory floor.

Jenny recognizes that these are symptoms of a stressed workforce. She concludes that the increased number of mistakes being picked up by quality control is related to employees' anxiety and fear about more job cuts. She knows that as manager, it's her duty to try to alleviate this stress.

Question

Which statements accurately describe signs of stress in employees?

Options:

1. Stressed employees tend to have more health complaints, which often leads to absenteeism

2. During periods of organizational change, employees may be fearful for their jobs and anxious about the future

3. When employees are making more mistakes in their work than usual, it can be a sign of stress

4. Employees who are stressed often only take it out on their coworkers or manager and avoid letting their negative feelings affect customers

5. Fear and anxiety are generally the only emotions associated with stressed employees

Answer

Option 1: This option is correct. When there is a rising incidence of employees complaining about health problems, that may be a sign that your workforce is experiencing excessive stress. These complaints may well escalate into an absenteeism issue.

Option 2: This option is correct. Employees who are stressed in times of organizational transition often display negative emotions such as fear and anxiety.

Option 3: This option is correct. Employees who are stressed can sometimes make more mistakes than they normally would, as the stress they're experiencing can make them less focused on their work.

Option 4: This option is incorrect. Employees can sometimes exhibit stress through negative emotions or comments directed at customers as well as colleagues and managers.

Option 5: This option is incorrect. Stressed employees also experience typical emotions of change, such as sadness and disbelief.

WAYS TO REDUCE STRESS

Ways to reduce stress

Not all stress is bad. Sometimes stress can be a good motivator, creating a necessary sense of urgency. But too much stress can adversely affect the health and productivity of employees. During periods of uncertainty and difficulty, you may yourself feel overwhelmed with duties and responsibilities, especially when resources are scarce. At such times, you should remember that employees will be experiencing frustration and stress too.

Before you can help your employees reduce their stress, you must be able to manage your own stress. And this is where time management techniques can be really useful. To alleviate your own stress, follow ur simple techniques. Establish priorities by distinguishing between important and urgent tasks. Be realistic about what you can achieve and how long it will take. Eliminate unnecessary interruptions from your work routine. And delegate suitable tasks to others where possible.

Establish priorities

A good way to reduce stress is to set priorities. You can organize your tasks in terms of importance and urgency. You might do the most difficult tasks first to avoid procrastination. Focus on doing one thing well before moving on to another. You may find that you're achieving more, and better quality, output as a result.

Be realistic

Being realistic about what you can achieve helps to lessen the stress you feel. To relieve pressure, don't always aim for perfection, but instead just do your best. Be realistic about time frames as well. If something needs a bit longer to get it right, then allow for this without putting extra strain on yourself.

Eliminate interruptions

Where possible, try to eliminate interruptions that prevent you from meeting the demands of your job. For instance, you may be able to cut out unnecessary meetings that prevent you from continuing with important tasks. But if interruptions are inevitable, try to develop methods for handling them to minimize their impact on your daily activities.

Delegate

Being an effective manager is not about doing everything yourself, but rather about having the ability to delegate tasks to the appropriate people. To reduce stress on yourself and on your workforce, try to balance the work to be done against the availability of people and skills.

Question

Which examples illustrate ways of managing time efficiently to reduce stress?

Options:

1. A team manager makes a list of tasks he needs to accomplish and then prioritizes by starting with the most important tasks first

2. During a period of change involving new product lines, a factory manager is careful not to be overly optimistic about how quickly the new lines can be introduced

3. During a downsizing phase, a department manager takes several days off to avoid questions about job losses and to cope with her workload

4. A stressed manager at a struggling secondhand car firm sets a goal for himself that he must exceed previous levels of profitability by 50%

Answer

Option 1: This option is correct. Establishing priorities among your tasks is an effective way to reduce stress levels.

Option 2: This option is correct. Being realistic about what can and can't be achieved is a good motivator and reducer of stress in times of change.

Option 3: This option is incorrect. While it's important to plan relaxation time, avoiding problems during change periods is not an effective coping strategy.

Option 4: This option is incorrect. The manager should reduce his stress by setting realistic goals and not aiming to be perfect, but rather to survive a rough patch.

Suppose you've succeeded in reducing your own stress as a manager in an organization that's going through difficult times. Now you can focus on your responsibility to reduce your employees' stress. There are three actions you can take to do this: keep track of people's workloads, help employees organize their work, and negotiate with your superiors for more resources when necessary.

First, be sure to keep track of employee workloads. This will help you to identify when an employee might be struggling. Incidentally, this will also reduce your own stress as a manager, as you'll feel more confident about where you are with regard to achieving goals.

When it comes to top performers, try to avoid the temptation to give them too many tasks. Otherwise you risk overwhelming them, and the efforts of the entire team will be undermined. As far as possible, spread out the workload evenly, and assign appropriate tasks to individuals.

Showing your awareness of individual workloads and adjusting these as necessary will considerably reduce employees' stress.

A second activity you can use to alleviate employee stress is help individuals organize their work. This is a critical part of a manager's job. For instance, it may be possible to eliminate low priority tasks completely during times of stress, or extend a deadline to reduce pressure on an overloaded employee. You can help employees to better organize their work in three ways: break large tasks into small, manageable steps; provide feedback on tangible results; and celebrate short-term wins.

Break tasks into manageable steps

Any successful strategy for helping employees organize their work involves breaking down large phases or tasks into smaller, more manageable ones. This allows employees to maintain a sense of control over their jobs and the change process. It reduces stress levels during tough times, as it creates a sense of achievement when each new smaller goal or objective is accomplished.

Provide feedback on results

When you provide feedback to employees on their progress, it will help reduce their stress. When an employee doesn't know how she's doing, that is in itself a stressor. Positive feedback on tangible results is also an antidote to the negative emotions that tend to surface due to excessive stress.

Celebrate short-term wins

In addition to providing regular feedback on the results that are being achieved, you should also celebrate small wins whenever possible. It's important to acknowledge and celebrate the passing of each milestone along the way. Stress tends to diminish employees' enthusiasm for the job and belief in the value of what you're doing, but by celebrating milestones, you keep spirits up and create a sense of moving closer to the higher goal.

A third strategy for relieving stress when your team is under pressure is to negotiate for more resources. In a large organization, you could suggest that parts of some projects be given to other departments to ease the pressure. Or you could suggest that some projects be set aside temporarily.

Consider this example. Paul is overseeing both the marketing and commercial elements of a new product launch, and he and his team are under a lot of pressure. He's concerned about falling behind on his regular strategic responsibilities, so he decides to discuss this with his superiors and negotiate for more resources.

Paul explains to his management team that there's been a lot of pressure on the Marketing and Commercial

Managing During Difficult Times

Departments related to researching and agreeing on price points for the new product range.

In order to take some of this pressure off, Paul gets his superiors' agreement that the Finance Department will take over this part of the launch. This frees up Paul's teams to concentrate their efforts on organizing the other elements of the launch.

Question

Which examples demonstrate how a manager can reduce employee stress during times of change?

Options:

1. A manager keeps a chart beside his desk that lists the current tasks and deadlines of each team member
2. A team leader helps one of her team members assess which of his tasks are urgent and which ones can be put on hold temporarily
3. A department head asks the director for permission to hire temporary help to relieve her team during preparation for a major conference
4. A manager tries to reduce stress on his team leading up to a deadline by giving extra tasks to two of the team's top performers
5. A manager tries to motivate an overloaded employee by refusing an extension on a deadline and insisting it will make him tougher in the end

Answer

Option 1: This option is correct. Keeping track of employees' workloads is a good way to reduce employee stress, as it informs you when employees are overloaded.

Option 2: This option is correct. Helping employees establish priorities regarding their work is a key skill managers can use to reduce occupational stress.

Option 3: This option is correct. Negotiating for more resources is a way of easing the pressure on your workforce during times of change or stress.

Option 4: This option is incorrect. It doesn't help to overload key performers. When they become stressed, it will eventually take its toll on the morale and productivity of the entire team.

Option 5: This option is incorrect. If employees are stressed, it's your job as a manager to help them organize their work by prioritizing what can and can't be done in a given period of time.

SECTION 2 - MOTIVATING EMPLOYEES IN CHANGING ORGANIZATIONS

SECTION 2 - Motivating Employees in Changing Organizations

There are a number of benefits to motivating employees during difficult times. It boosts performance, helps avoid excessive absenteeism and the spread of negativity, improves intracompany relations, and fosters an environment that's more conducive to creativity.

There are several general guidelines you can use to develop your own motivational management style during such times. You need to deliberately focus on employee motivation, be an example by becoming highly motivated yourself, communicate often, and foster a positive organizational culture.

THE BENEFITS OF MOTIVATING EMPLOYEES

The benefits of motivating employees

During periods of organizational challenge, the ability to keep employees motivated and productive is one of the greatest skills a leader can possess. The challenge could be a merger, a downsizing or expansion initiative, economic pressures, or even a wide-scale process overhaul, such as the introduction of new IT systems. But regardless of the cause, keeping the workforce motivated is vital at such times.

Frustration and worry – the negative effects of change – are often rife among employees in these circumstances. The big challenge for managers is to keep their employees motivated and engaged during such periods. If companies can manage the difficult times effectively, they can emerge from them in a stronger position than before. Managers must create a positive spirit and increase employee engagement to ensure workers don't focus on the negative.

Consider this example. A medium-sized company that manufactures medical devices has been experiencing economic pressures and has recently introduced a hiring freeze. The reason for the difficulties is a new drug that doctors are using more and more of in place of the more invasive devices that the company manufactures.

The company's CEO, Luke, wants to increase motivation levels among employees. Although the company is under a lot of strain, Luke's efforts will benefit the company's ability to survive this tough phase. Luke knows that increasing motivation levels will help to maximize performance, avoid excessive absenteeism, and avoid the spread of negative attitudes. It also helps to improve relations among the workforce and it contributes to the company's competitive advantage by encouraging employees to generate new ideas and improve the organization.

Maximize performance

Luke knows that maximizing performance levels is always important, but is especially vital when times are economically tough. As Luke applies strategies to increase motivation and morale, productivity increases, which helps the company both in its new research and in servicing its existing orders more efficiently.

Avoid excessive absenteeism

When the company first began experiencing difficulties, Luke noticed a rise in levels of absenteeism, which was reducing productivity. As Luke begins to apply effective motivational strategies, he notices that absenteeism falls. The employees now feel more engaged and like an integral part of the company-wide change.

Avoid spread of negative attitudes

Luke's techniques have improved morale, which helps to prevent the spread of negative attitudes. When a small number of less motivated employees spread negativity, it can have a detrimental effect on the entire company. By improving engagement and motivation, Luke is working toward preventing this as much as possible.

Improve relations

As the workforce becomes more enthusiastic about the company's efforts to survive and make changes, it inevitably helps to improve relations within the company. This in turn leads to higher efficiency and improved morale, both of which help to ease Luke's company through difficult times.

Generate new ideas and improve relations

Luke implements an initiative that encourages new ideas to improve the company. He notices that increased engagement levels have led to employees approaching him with ideas for making things more efficient, as well as suggestions for entirely new products and services. Some of the ideas may prove to be extremely significant as the company reconsiders its position in the market.

Question

What are the benefits of increasing employee motivation during challenging times for your organization?

Options:

1. Helps employees improve their performance
2. May reduce absenteeism
3. Helps foster more positive attitudes
4. Can help people get along better within the organization
5. Supports a better climate for creativity within the company
6. Ensures the success of the transitional phase

Managing During Difficult Times

7. Prepares employees for all future changes

Answer

Option 1: This option is correct. Motivating employees significantly helps to keep performance levels up, which is critical during difficult times.

Option 2: This option is correct. Absenteeism is harmful at any time, but particularly when it tends to increase during tough times. Motivating employees helps to avoid this.

Option 3: This option is correct. Motivating the workforce helps to avoid a situation where less motivated employees negatively affect the motivation of other employees in the company.

Option 4: This option is correct. By increasing motivation levels, internal company relations are improved and morale is boosted.

Option 5: This option is correct. Staff members who are more motivated often have new ideas that can help the company during times of transition.

Option 6: This option is incorrect. Boosting employee motivation can make implementing a change initiative go more smoothly, but it cannot guarantee the success of the initiative.

Option 7: This option is incorrect. Motivating your workforce is not a one-time effort, but rather an ongoing process that becomes even more critical during any challenging time.

DEVELOPING A MOTIVATIONAL STYLE

Developing a motivational style

As a manager, you should be aware of the importance of motivating your team. Sometimes it can be hard to know how to do this, especially when the organization is going through a period of upheaval. But there are four guidelines that can help you develop a motivational leadership style that can be applied in all such circumstances: remember to focus on motivating employees, be an example to your employees, communicate often with them, and foster a positive organizational culture.

The first thing is to pay attention to whether your employees are motivated or not. You may have lost sight of this while concentrating on your managerial tasks, but you need to regain this focus.

Try to check up on staff motivation levels regularly. For example, you could keep a diary for recording your team's motivation levels on a weekly or monthly basis. In addition, you could keep a list of motivational actions that you know from experience work best for your team.

Make time for activities to boost morale in your daily and weekly task planning. And where possible, try to add a fun aspect to people's jobs. For example, you could invite your team for coffee once a week to allow for a little downtime and friendly conversation.

A second way to motivate those you lead is by setting an example yourself. Be optimistic about opportunities and possibilities in your conversations with employees. You can't expect them to have a positive attitude if you don't project one yourself.

Take Richard, a manager at an office supply company. He meets with his employees each week to discuss projects and gauge how motivated people are. If motivation levels seem to be falling, he organizes a staff night out, which can be relied on to boost morale.

Richard also maintains an upbeat attitude when he chats with employees in the warehouse and the store. He tries to maintain an element of fun and optimism in the workplace by encouraging suggestions for the next company night out.

To help you become a motivational example for your team, reignite your own passion for what you do. One way to do that is to create or revise your personal mission statement and vision to remind yourself what motivates you about your job. Then you could have a vision session with your team at a comfortable location.

Another key aspect of setting a good example for your team is being honest with them. Never try to conceal problems. However, make sure you avoid being dominated by negative thoughts.

Question

A new product development manager is overseeing the merger of her department with the Marketing Department. What techniques can she use to keep her employees motivated through the period of change?

Options:

1. Keep a diary to help check the motivational levels of her team on a weekly basis

2. Include motivational and fun activities in her planning of weekly tasks

3. Be optimistic about opportunities and possibilities that the merger will bring about for her team and the company

4. Focus on immediate problems rather than wider goals

5. Encourage employees to discuss the negative aspects of the merger in the hope that they'll see how few there are

6. Be honest with members of both departments about the sacrifices that will need to be made during the change and about the reasons for the change

Answer

Option 1: This option is correct. Having somewhere to regularly record your impressions of your team's morale is one way to keep you focused on employee motivation. Paying attention is the first step toward improving employee motivation.

Option 2: This option is correct. Making time for motivational tasks and adding fun to people's jobs are good ways to boost morale among your employees.

Managing During Difficult Times

Option 3: This option is correct. Setting an example by focusing on the positives of the situation is a powerful way to motivate employees during challenging times.

Option 4: This option is incorrect. It's important to keep your eye on your wider goals and vision while still dealing with immediate problems.

Option 5: This option is incorrect. It's important not to turn away from problems, but it's also best to avoid negative influences wherever possible in order to keep motivation levels up.

Option 6: This option is correct. It's OK to allude to challenges that employees will face during transition periods, as long as you're honest. Employees will feel less stressed if they know what to expect and the reasons behind the changes they're experiencing.

A third way of increasing motivation is to communicate often with employees, particularly during large-scale changes. You can do this by celebrating short-term wins to boost levels of confidence in the

workforce and re-energize commitment to the change effort. For example, you could congratulate teams or individuals publicly for achievements, using company meetings or newsletters. You could even present certificates or small rewards to create a sense of accomplishment.

You should also give regular, relevant feedback. Maybe you've conducted a survey or solicited employees' opinions in some other way. If so, you must give feedback to show how you've taken account of their views.

Employees will be more motivated if they feel like they're an integral part of the organization, and like they're being kept up-to-date on information that affects them and the company.

During turbulent times, employees may find it hard to take important information in, so try to give useful information frequently. To alleviate their anxiety, make sure employees are empowered by having the relevant information. For example, if layoffs have to be made, try to give as much timely information as possible about when the cuts will be made and the criteria the company is using to make the cuts.

Providing feedback helps increase motivation levels in a number of ways. First, it increases employee engagement, as feedback means employees are more aware of the results of their work and what's going on in general. Second, it helps high performers thrive, as knowing relevant information creates a sense of accomplishment and empowerment. Finally, it reinforces employees' focus.

Increases employee engagement

In order to motivate employees, you have to make sure they can trust you. Employees become more engaged in their work when they receive regular, positive feedback. When employees are aware of the effects their efforts are having on the overall success of the company, they feel a sense of belonging and are more motivated as a result.

Helps high performers thrive

High performers in particular tend to thrive on feedback because they like to know where they stand, what effect their efforts are having on the company as a whole, and what they can do to improve. The more feedback you give, the better results you'll achieve from all members of your team.

Reinforces employees' focus

Managing During Difficult Times

In uncertain times, feedback is critical because employees need to know they're focusing on the right things and that their performance is adding value. It can be hard to hold on to the best-performing employees, as they're often the ones who'll leave first if their skills are underutilized.

Providing regular, relevant feedback helps keep employees focused on their work and helps retain valuable employees.

Question

Which scenarios demonstrate using communication to reduce employee stress during times of organizational change or difficulty?

Options:

1. A manager calls a workforce meeting to announce a number of organizational milestones the company has reached in the last six months

2. Following a company-wide survey, employees are given information about the changes that are being introduced in response to their suggestions

3. During a complicated merger, the communications officer for a large company keeps employees up to date on imminent changes via emails

4. During a period of change, a stressed manager tells his employees that there's going to be a very tough time ahead for everyone

5. During a time of economic difficulty, a department head cautions her team that they shouldn't get too comfortable, despite having recently received a prestigious industry award

Answer

Option 1: This option is correct. Communicating with employees by celebrating short-term wins is an excellent way to reduce stress and boost morale.

Option 2: This option is correct. If opinions are solicited from employees during times of change, it's vital that you provide feedback explaining how the information is being used and how they'll benefit from providing suggestions.

Option 3: This option is correct. To reduce employee stress during times of large-scale change, it's important to provide regular, relevant information.

Option 4: This option is incorrect. It's important to give employees honest, relevant information to reduce stress, but this should only be done when you can be specific about the challenges you expect.

Option 5: This option is incorrect. While it's important to be realistic with your employees during difficult times, you should try to reduce stress and boost morale by celebrating short-term wins.

The fourth way you can improve your motivational management style is by fostering a positive organizational culture. There are two aspects to implementing this strategy: empowering employees and focusing on high performance.

Empowering employees helps to foster a positive culture. Staff members feel more motivated when they understand the power they have to make a difference in the organization. They become focused on what they're offering the company, as well as what they're getting from it.

You can empower your workforce by recognizing and rewarding them for their efforts. Show that good performance is appreciated and poor performance is not. This involves clearly defining what does and doesn't count as good performance. Employees will feel that their efforts are noticed and respond with a more motivated attitude and higher productivity. For example, a simple way to recognize efforts could involve acknowledging individual or team achievements at company meetings or in corporate newsletters.

Another way to empower employees is to provide clarity and direction. This is particularly important during uncertain times. By connecting top performers with the organization's "big picture," the focus of the company becomes the focus of its employees as well.

Try to ensure employees have the knowledge and resources they need to fulfill their roles properly. When employees receive clear guidance and direction, they understand how their efforts make a genuine difference to the organization as a whole. For example, you could schedule regular catch-up calls with employees to ensure they're clear about what they're currently working on and have everything they need to accomplish it.

Also, try to listen more attentively to employees' ideas and concerns. Encourage open and honest dialogue so that staff members know their thoughts are valued by the company.

If an organization is to remain competitive, focusing on good performance should become one of its core values. This is critical for maintaining employee commitment and engagement, and for fostering a positive culture. Goal setting and good communication help establish the right values and attitudes among employees for a more productive workplace. Building trust and accountability also help to sustain a strong and positive culture.

Goal setting

You should aim to set and then link goals to the mission and strategy of the organization so that employees understand the contributions they're making to the wider effort.

For example, a manager could remind his team that the project they're currently working on will help the company to achieve its goal of moving into a new market in the next six months. He can motivate the team by pointing out that their work will directly influence the vision of creating several new jobs and boosting annual profits.

Good communication

It's important to use good communication at all times. Don't forget to also use nonverbal techniques, such as body language and tone of voice. Ensure you clearly establish the expectations and positive standards that shape the company and team cultures.

For example, a manager who responds in a calm, positive tone to problems and exudes confidence in her body language will instill the same confidence and positive attitude in her team.

Trust

As a manager, building trust is vital for maintaining a positive culture. To boost a positive culture, remember to always honor your commitments and own up to mistakes.

For example, a manager who always turns up to staff gatherings regardless of how busy she is, will be trusted by employees more and seen as reliable.

Accountability

When every team member is accountable and responsibilities are shared, the team buys into the company culture. Morale, excitement, and the desire to achieve boost performance, and it becomes much easier to sustain a positive attitude throughout the culture as a result.

For example, a manager who takes responsibility for his own mistakes and isn't afraid to take on extra work for the team helps to boost motivation levels and encourage similar input from all team members.

Question

Match the examples of actions to the corresponding principles for developing an effective motivational management style.

Options:

A. A manager makes time for motivational activities and tries to add fun aspects to the working environment

B. A team leader rewrites her own vision and mission statement to reignite her passion for her work

C. A regional retail manager overseeing a large-scale expansion uses weekly e-mails to inform employees when targets have been met

D. A store manager introduces a system of reward and recognition to refocus employees on their contributions and on high performance

Targets:

1. Focus on employee motivation
2. Be an example
3. Communicate often
4. Foster a positive organizational culture

Answer

Sorin Dumitrascu

Increasing your focus on employee motivation by adding fun aspects to people's everyday routines, is an effective motivational technique during times of change.

If you aim to be an example by readdressing your vision and mission statement, your motivation and focus will influence those you manage as well.

In order to motivate staff during times of change, it's important to communicate often by giving them useful information frequently.

Reward and recognition and focusing on high performance are both effective ways of increasing motivation by fostering a positive organizational culture.

SECTION 3 - SUPPORTING EMPLOYEES THROUGH DIFFICULT TIMES

SECTION 3 - Supporting Employees through Difficult Times

During times of large-scale organizational change, employees may experience a variety of emotional reactions. As a manager, one of the most important skills you can have is the ability to manage these reactions.

There are two strategies you can use to do this: acknowledge what employees are experiencing, and give them permission to react. You can acknowledge employees' situations by letting them know you understand and appreciate their efforts. And you can grant them permission to react by allowing for the variety of reactions you might experience.

There are also three overarching principles that should apply to all your interactions during times of change: be calm, be realistic, and be positive.

SUPPORTING EMPLOYEES IN DIFFICULT TIMES

Supporting employees in difficult times

As a manager, have you been confused about how to help your team through difficult times? There are two principles you can apply when communicating support to stressed employees: acknowledge employees' experience, and give them permission to react. When acknowledging their experience, try to show that you understand the stress they're under. When giving permission to react, you should allow employees to vent their feelings in reaction to difficult times. This is necessary if communication is to be honest.

There are also three overarching principles that should govern all your communications with employees: always be calm, realistic, and positive.

For example, suppose your company is experiencing financial difficulty and has to introduce some cost-cutting measures. These measures won't be popular, but it certainly won't help the employees cope if you communicate the news in a panic-stricken way, strike a doom-and-gloom tone, and make unrealistic promises about the future.

Better to stay calm, explain what's going on and why the temporary cuts are necessary, and point out how the strategy will benefit the company in the long run.

During times of large-scale change, employees are disrupted from their usual routines and often feel unsure about their roles or new tasks that have been assigned to them. This creates a sense of anxiety among the workforce and employees may feel isolated as they struggle to adjust. There are two ways you can acknowledge employees' feelings of stress: let them know you understand what they're going through, and show that you appreciate their efforts.

Let them know you understand

The more employees feel understood and cared for, the better they'll be able to contribute to a healthier work environment. By demonstrating that you empathize with them, you'll make them feel calmer and more positive about what's going on. Showing you understand makes staff members feel they're supported and not alone in their efforts to adjust.

Appreciate their efforts

Recognition and encouragement contribute greatly toward keeping a company competitive during challenging times. Remember to thank your team for the extra efforts they're making in response to organizational problems or change. If staff members feel appreciated, they'll be much more enthusiastic about putting in extra effort to make transitions as smooth as possible.

Harry is the manager of a bookstore. In the last few years, the business has begun to struggle because of the increasing availability of online and digital books and data. But Harry knows how valuable his experienced and knowledgeable staff are to the business. Follow along as he acknowledges the situation and shows appreciation for the efforts of an employee, Sylvia.

Harry: I know you're probably anxious about the recent layoffs. Just so you know, I have plans for this place and you're part of them.

Harry says calmly

Sylvia: What a relief...do I ever appreciate hearing that! Sounds exciting! How can I help?

Sylvia is relieved and enthused.

Harry: You already have. I'm using your idea to diversify into selling digital books and then promote the wealth of knowledge we have on-staff. I want customers to see us as a reference point when they need information and suggestions. Thank you for such a great idea!

Harry is enthusiastic.

Sylvia: Wow...you're using my suggestion! You know, I have a few other ideas, if you're interested...

Sylvia is excited.

By acknowledging the fallout from the layoffs, Harry actually made Sylvia feel more secure in her job and appreciative of his honesty and consideration.

Harry also supported Sylvia by thanking her for her idea and by acknowledging how valuable she is to the company. Sylvia now feels appreciated and supported, which makes her much more motivated and excited about the future.

Question

Managing During Difficult Times

Which statements represent examples of what managers might say to acknowledge what employees are experiencing during times of change?

Options:

1. "I'm sure you must be feeling a little anxious about the recent changes we've made here."
2. "I know it's been a tough few months lately, but I want to thank you for all your hard work. We really couldn't survive without it."
3. "It's been tough around here lately, but a little bit of hard work won't do you any harm. You had it quite easy for a long time."
4. "It's been a tough time lately for us here, but you don't seem bothered by it too much."

Answer

Option 1: This option is correct. It opens up a discussion by acknowledging what the employee is probably feeling but may be afraid to express voluntarily to a manager.

Option 2: This option is correct. Showing employees that you recognize and appreciate their efforts is a way of implicitly acknowledging what they're going through as the company experiences turbulent times.

Option 3: This option is incorrect. Making light of employee efforts will only serve to undermine their motivation.

Option 4: This option is incorrect. You shouldn't assume that employees are fine just because they don't express feelings of anxiety or fear.

It's important when supporting employees through difficult times that you give them permission to react– that is, you need to accept that emotions can be intense at times like this and be patient with each other. You also need to "normalize" employee reactions. Among the typical phases employees go through in response to job upheaval are denial, resistance, and acceptance. In some cases, there's a period of exploration before reaching the acceptance or commitment phase of the new situation.

In sequence, select each phase of typical employee reactions to change to learn more about it.

Denial

In the denial phase, employees may handle change by pretending it's not happening. They may adopt an attitude that assumes the change won't really happen or that it will go away if they just don't think about it.

Resistance

Once employees have moved beyond denial, they may react by strongly resisting change. This attitude might be reflected in thoughts like, "I'm not going to make any extra effort if I'm not getting extra money or rewards in return for it."

Acceptance

Eventually, employees may reach a phase of accepting the new situation and seeing the positives in it. For example, they may adopt the attitude, "If I put in the extra effort now when the company needs it most, I'll be appreciated more and may get a promotion down the line."

Consider this example. Teresa is the owner and manager of a large jewelry and gift store that has recently experienced a decline in sales. As a result, Teresa has announced that she'll have to lay off two sales assistants and restructure her business and product line. Follow along as she discusses the changes with an employee, Anthony.

Teresa: How are you handling all this recent news?
Teresa questions

Anthony: I'm not too worried. I think everybody will get used to it, eventually.
Anthony is unconcerned

Teresa: I like your positive attitude, but it is going to be different around here. I had no choice but to make the layoffs. I'm also going to have to get rid of the home and giftware sections, and then consider some new areas I can diversify into. We'll get through it, though, by helping each other.
Teresa say calmly

Anthony: I do feel bad about the layoffs, but I guess that happens, huh?
Anthony is inquisitive.

Teresa: Yes, unfortunately it does. It's all a pretty big change, and it'll be bumpy for all of us for a while. But I think you have what it takes to move forward.
Teresa explains reassuringly

Anthony: Wow, thanks for the vote of confidence! I'm actually looking forward to the changes now!
Anthony is enthused

Early on in the conversation, Anthony appears to be in denial about how significant the changes are and the impact they'll have on him and the company.

Teresa allows for his reaction of denial and doesn't bombard him with information that will scare him. Instead, she gently alludes to the challenges they face and reassures him about how he'll cope. Anthony seems ready to move from denial to a stage of motivated commitment by the end of the conversation.

Question

Which statements demonstrate managers giving employees permission to react?

Options:

1. "I understand your attitude toward the change. We can all help each other out when we need support."

2. "I can see that you're struggling to adjust, it's been quite manic here lately. But don't worry that's why I'm here to help you."

3. "I don't see why you're still resisting. It's time you just accept it."

4. "Why are you so angry and upset about the news? You're overreacting. No one else is behaving that way."

Answer

Option 1: This option is correct. It's a statement that reassures the employee that the reaction is fine, regardless of whether it's denial or resistance.

Option 2: This option is correct. You are allowing the employee to react by seeing things from their point of view and then reassuring them it's going to be ok.

Option 3: This option is incorrect. There are times you may need to help employees move through a stage of reaction by giving extra support and avoiding criticism.

Option 4: This option is incorrect. You need to allow employees to react, even if you feel they're overreacting.

REFERENCES

References

Corporate Conversations: Guide to Crafting Effective and Appropriate Internal Communications - 2004, Shel Holtz, AMACOM

How to Manage People - 2008, Michael Armstrong, Kogan Page

Chaotics: The Business of Managing and Marketing in the Age of Turbulence - 2009, Philip Kotler and John A. Caslione, AMACOM

Tough Tactics for Tough Times: How To Maintain Business Success in Difficult Economic Conditions - 2009, Patrick Forsyth and Frances Kay, Kogan Page

The Headcount Solution: How to Cut Compensation Costs and Keep Your Best People - 2003, N. Fredric Crandall and Marc J. Wallace , McGraw-Hill

**The Happy Employee: 101 Ways For Managers To Attract, Retain, & Inspire The Best And

Brightest - 2008, Julia McGovern & Susan Shelly, Adams Media

Corporate Conversations: Guide to Crafting Effective and Appropriate Internal Communications - 2004, Shel Holtz, AMACOM

GLOSSARY

Glossary
B
business plan - A formal statement of business goals and the plans for reaching them.
C
communications plan - A method of communicating key messages to employees and other stakeholders in relation to changes to an organization's strategy or goal.
compensation - Something given as an equivalent for services, debt, loss or injury.
O
organizational culture - The shared values, beliefs, and behaviors among employees in an organization.
outplacement services - Assistance provided to individuals being laid off to help them get new jobs, such as providing references and compiling and distributing employee resumes to appropriate employers.
R

resource - Any sources or supplies that support business objectives.

resume book - A compilation of resumes used to help employees being laid off get new jobs.

S

staff-related expenses - Expenses incurred by having employees, including compensation and benefits.

strategic alliance - In business, a relationship between two or more parties to pursue agreed-upon goals.

strategy - A plan to obtain a specific goal or result.

tactics - Actions taken to execute a desired outcome.

www.ingramcontent.com/pod-product-compliance
Lightning Source LLC
Chambersburg PA
CBHW020918180526
45163CB00007B/2793